Take Care of

Phoebe

BUILDING AUTHENTIC SISTAH RELATIONSHIPS

DR. LAWANNA HARROD

Published by Harrod Publishing
Clinton, Maryland 20735
(240) 244-6502

Printed in the United States
Library of Congress

Table of Contents

Dedication

This is dedicated to all women who will trust God for new seasons of authentic relationships.

One of our greatest challenges is learning to trust one another in friendship. This book delves into the transformative hopes and joys that arise when we intentionally open our hearts to each other. By inviting others to join us at the table, we create opportunities for authentic connections, support, and a shared celebration of our journeys.

I am confident that you will feel inspired to actively seek out and nurture meaningful and lasting friendships. Each connection offers an opportunity to build deep relationships that can greatly enhance our lives. These friendships provide companionship and unwavering support, helping us navigate the complexities and challenges we face on our journey through life.

As we embark on this journey of building authentic friendships, I encourage you to fully embrace each moment. Engage in heartfelt conversations, share your experiences, and create memories that will last a lifetime. You will be amazed at how these relationships flourish and transform into something truly beautiful, resilient, and meaningful. By investing in these connections, we set the stage for a rich tapestry of emotions, laughter, and shared growth that can sustain us through triumphs and challenges. Remember, half the battle is simply showing up.

Forward

I am thoroughly convinced that every woman needs a Sistah friend, a Sistah girl, a Sistah or two, or a few life-giving connections in her life. Dr. Lawanna Harrod defines the meaning of this Sistahhood bond and blessed dynamic in her book, *Take Care of Phoebe*. You are encouraged to embrace those who QUALIFY into your world, sphere, and circle with access to this lofty and sacred place. Sistahs are companions of a different realm, and all do not rise to the place of admission, as Dr. Lawanna expounds on the qualities of a true Sistah.

I wrestle immediately with why I should be assigned, requested, or tasked to take care of Phoebe when viewing the title. Here, within these 23 chapters, the answer is fully disclosed. In chapter one, Dr. Lawanna begins this dialogue with a broad glimpse into a true Sistah's face, character, and role. Then she carefully takes you into a full-blown stare, face to face, eye to eye, elongated view of Phoebe, the Sistah we should emulate in everyday life. The context of *Take Care of Phoebe*, in truth, is the reciprocal command to take care of those needful, holistic, vital relationships of Sistahs who take care of you and nourish your soul. The call to attention is to extend and/or create more than transactional relationships. It's about nurturing real-lationships, authentic, mutually edifying, sharing, building, and being....

The world is almost bankrupt from true wealth in loyal, lasting, healthy, integral, personal relationships. Hence, the value of true friendship is not to be underestimated. It's a real treasure and a rare find. Dr. Lawanna, as a vested broker, brings you to the table and reviews the risks and rewards of taking the chance to embrace deep friendships, specifically to recover if you tried and were disappointed at prior outcomes; how to read the warning signs of toxic friendships and how to dismiss the unhealthy with practical steps to end these without guilt or remorse. She shares sober advice and assistance to discover greater possibilities when you let go and go beyond conflicted perspectives.

I commend this book to you for your reading, inspiration, and instruction. I trust the content and the author, this Phoebe woman. Dr Lawanna is a Sistah, my Sistah friend for over 30 years. For the last four decades, her work has been creating community and harmony and building a platform for women's voices. True and tried in the trenches of life, she writes with insight emerging from her own encounters and experiences, losses and gains, lessons and life. You will benefit from this reading, be challenged, and be encouraged to intentionally cultivate and continue authentic, transformative Sistah-to-Sistah friendships. We all need to take care of Phoebe. It is the essence of caring for our soul.

Dr. Lisa R Hickman

Life Enrichment Ministries
Atlanta, GA

Accolade

In a world where the complexities of life often overshadow the simple joys, *Take Care of Phoebe* emerges as a poignant reminder of the profound connections that exist between us. This heartfelt narrative invites readers to journey through the intricacies of love, responsibility, and the bittersweet nature of growing up.

At its core, the story revolves around Phoebe, a character whose experiences resonate with anyone who has ever felt the weight of expectation and the longing for acceptance. Through her eyes, we are reminded of the delicate balance between caring for others and nurturing our own identities. This tale captures the essence of what it means to truly "take care"—not just of those we love, but also of ourselves.

The author deftly weaves themes of friendship, family, and self-discovery into a tapestry that is both relatable and inspiring. Each page unfolds with warmth and empathy, inviting readers to reflect on their own relationships and the impact they have on one another. The narrative is rich with moments of vulnerability and strength, illustrating that it is often through our struggles that we find clarity and purpose.

As you dive into *Take Care of Phoebe*, allow yourself to be immersed in its world. Embrace the laughter, the tears, and the transformative power of connection. This book is not just a story; it is an invitation to examine how we care for one another and appreciate the beauty in the journey of growth.

So, settle in, open your heart, and prepare to be touched by Phoebe's journey. The pages ahead mirror our lives, urging us to reflect on what it truly means to take care of someone— or something—precious.

Enjoy the journey.

Dr. Joan A. Miller

Christ Cathedral of Praise
Statesville, NC

Sistah

A Sistah is someone who will bring
comfort, peace, and laughter.

A Sistah is someone who will lift your spirit
when you're feeling down and out for the count.

A Sistah is someone who will connect the threads of life
and walk alongside you even in your dark dry places.

A Sistah is someone who will fill your life with meaning,
purpose, and love.

A Sistah is someone who will stand and fight for you and
ask questions later.

My Sistah is my friend; she is my Phoebe

Dr. LaWanna Harrod

Chapter One

OPPORTUNITY

I had the opportunity to present at SisterCare International's Women By Revelation Conference in 1997, which was expertly directed by Dr. Verlean Hailey. My presentation focused on the theme *"Connecting With Phoebe,"* where I explored the importance of building meaningful relationships.

A diverse and inspiring group of women gathered for an engaging seminar focused on the significance of building authentic relationships in our everyday lives, with an eye toward the coming year. This event was crafted to be both intensive and interactive, encouraging participants to step outside their comfort zones and connect with individuals they had not met before.

The conference attendees received clear and thoughtful instructions on how to connect with one another during the event. They were encouraged to use various methods of communication after the conference, such as phone calls, text messages, emails, and instant messaging. The emphasis was on fostering connections that would extend beyond the event itself, as this was a goal for the entire year.

By fostering these ongoing connections, the seminar aimed to strengthen our bonds and ensure that the valuable discussions and insights shared during the conference would remain active and impactful long after the event concluded. Ultimately, this approach was designed for the participants to sustain the momentum of support and growth in their lives.

Phoebe Charlene Ndi

I connected with Charlene Ndi at the conference, and my journey with her has been truly remarkable. Over the years, I have faced many challenges that have tested my resilience and faith. During those tough times, I often paused to listen for the Lord's still, small voice, which provided gentle guidance and reassurance. When I chose to follow that prompting, it was almost like clockwork—my phone would ring, and it would be Charlene reaching out to me.

Charlene took the time to listen to my struggles. Whether I was facing a personal crisis or experiencing moments of doubt, she offered comforting perspectives that illuminated the path ahead. After sharing my thoughts with her, I always ended our calls feeling uplifted, as she brought strength and peace to my journey. I cherish every conversation with her; we always concluded our calls with shared laughter, which helped dissolve the weight of my worries. We made a heartfelt promise to reconnect soon, strengthening our bond and heightening our anticipation for the following uplifting conversation.

I picked up my pen and paper, writing frantically-afraid I would quickly forget the words I so clearly heard the Lord speak to my heart.

"Take a moment to notice and appreciate the people you encounter on your journey. Each individual has a unique story and perspective that contributes to your experiences. Acknowledging their significance can enhance your understanding of the world and help you build stronger connections. In this season, I will fill

the voids with Myself, and you should lay aside every burden. This connection comes from Me."

After finishing my prayer, I felt a new sense of awareness and anticipation. I began to reflect on the different individuals I might encounter and the significant roles they could play in my life. My mind raced with countless scenarios and possibilities, each one more vivid and intriguing than the last. Would I meet a wise mentor who could offer invaluable guidance, or perhaps someone with a fresh perspective who could challenge my current path? The anticipation of these potential meetings sparked my imagination and filled me with curiosity about the connections that awaited me. I remained open to these experiences.

LEANING IN

"This is amazing," I whispered to myself as I locked eyes with Charlene at the conference. Her expression showed genuine interest. Instead of taking the empty seat assigned to me, I felt an irresistible urge to lean into this unexpected connection. I settled into the chair beside her, subtly adjusting my posture to face her fully.

As the presentation faded into the background, we effortlessly moved beyond the usual conference small talk. Our conversation flowed freely, touching on experiences that had shaped our lives and dreams that sparkled like distant stars, waiting to be achieved. It felt as though we were old friends reconnecting after years apart, with the comfort of familiarity enveloping us like a warm blanket.

We shared our stories and discussed how we ended up here. She recounted her thrilling adventures while I talked about the challenges I faced. Each story enriched our conversation, illustrating our journeys.

I appreciated the beauty of our connection. It is powerful to use our voices to share the stories of others, especially those we may not know well. In those moments, we uncover the common threads of our humanity, weaving a rich tapestry of understanding and empathy.

I realized the importance of our meeting; we were present, listened to each other, and were open to trying new things. This is how we build meaningful friendships. After our encounter, I felt warm, content, and satisfied with this connection.

An Unexpected Visit

Charlene approached me with a sense of purpose and a fierce determination that was hard to ignore. Her eyes sparkled with confidence and insight, and I quickly sensed that she had an uncanny ability to see beyond the surface. It didn't take long for me to realize that she was well-acquainted with the shadow of my inner friend—my persistent companion of low self-esteem. Anxiety mingled with hope-filled my chest, and my heart skipped a beat as I caught her gaze. This encounter took on a depth I hadn't anticipated, becoming increasingly intriguing and layered with meaning. As I sat there, the Lord's tender instruction echoed in my mind, resonating with palpable clarity and warmth as if guiding me through this unexpected moment of connection and reflection.

PAY ATTENTION. PAY ATTENTION

After a few minutes of engaging conversation, we finally found common ground, leading us to a moment of tranquility. It became clear that this connection we formed marked the beginning of something authentic and meaningful. I found it somewhat unsettling yet fascinating to realize just how at ease I felt with Charlene when, a short while ago, we had been strangers, and now, in this brief time, we were sharing personal goals, stories, laughter, and prayer, as if we had known each other for years. The rapid shift from unfamiliarity to comfort was surprising and reassuring, hinting at the potential for deeper relationships to flourish from this encounter. This Phoebe Connection started about 28 years ago.

We visited each other in Baltimore, where she worked as a nurse. She often shared stories about her family, job, and goals. It became clear to me that our seemingly chance encounter at the conference was anything but accidental. It was a divine meeting with the One who guides our steps.

When we dedicate ourselves fully, without distractions, we offer the most generous gift to others—a connection that touches the heart and fosters a deeper bond. These connections unite people and create *meaningful friendships* where there were previously none.

As we lean in, we are moved from mere interaction to authentic connection. How might our lives change if we fully commit to listening to and sharing one another's stories?

When someone shares their personal story, they offer a profound invitation to engage with something significant and important. This storytelling is not merely a recounting of events but a revelation of their innermost self—sharing experiences, emotions, and insights that shape who they are. In presenting their narrative, they display a remarkable level of vulnerability, exposing their thoughts and feelings in a way that invites empathy and understanding.

By sharing their story, they ask us to recognize and appreciate the weight of their experiences. This is not just an opportunity to listen; it is a call to honor the sacredness of their truth. We are urged to treat their narrative with the utmost respect, mindful of the trust they place in us by revealing such intimate details of their lives. It is vital to approach their story with care and sensitivity, avoiding the temptation to dismiss or take it lightly.

This act of sharing also requires us to actively engage in the process of understanding and valuing what has been offered. We must commit ourselves to listening attentively and nurturing and protecting the essence of their story, recognizing the bravery it takes to lay such profound personal experiences before us. Ultimately, we gain an opportunity for connection, insight, and growth through our respect and reverence for their shared journey.

Being vulnerable and open requires courage. Exposing your true self to others can feel daunting, but this transparency serves as an essential pathway to building genuine intimacy. When we allow ourselves to be seen, flaws and all, we create an environment where deeper, more meaningful friendships can flourish. It's a process that invites trust and understanding.

Moreover, listening plays a crucial role in this dynamic and involves risk. Engaging with someone on a deeper level means opening ourselves up to their thoughts, feelings, and experiences, which can be challenging. However, this active listening reinforces connections and helps cultivate a safe space for mutual vulnerability, ultimately enriching our relationships and enhancing our sense of community.

The true art of *listening* to one another extends beyond merely hearing words; it involves fully engaging our hearts and emotions. Listening attentively creates a space where feelings, thoughts, and vulnerabilities can be shared freely. This deep level of understanding and connection is crucial because the heart, with all its complexities, is a delicate and fragile entity. Care, empathy, and genuine presence are required to foster meaningful communication and build strong relationships. Embracing this holistic approach to listening can transform interactions, allowing us to truly connect on a profound level.

This type of *listening* goes beyond mere responses; it aims for profound understanding. It involves truly *hearing* the emotional heartbeat beneath the surface, seeking to connect with the essence of the individual speaking. This practice demands courage and a willingness to delve deep into the complexities of human emotions. It is not for those who shy away from vulnerability, as it requires confronting uncomfortable truths and embracing the rawness of genuine human experience. Only through such brave engagement can we foster deeper connections and empathy.

Some stories shared through this Phoebe connect can be challenging to listen to, stirring emotions we may have buried deep within ourselves. These narratives might compel us to engage in a profound journey of self-reflection, prompting us to confront feelings and thoughts we have long overlooked or tried to ignore. As we absorb these tales, we might grapple with painful memories or uncomfortable truths, awakening thoughts and emotions that had grown numb over time. In this way, specific stories have the power to ignite a spark within our souls, rekindling a sense of awareness and connection to our own experiences and those of others. This awakening can lead to personal growth and a deeper understanding of the human experience.

HOLINESS IN THE PRESENT

I sat quietly, fully engrossed in the stories the women around me shared, each resonating deeply within my heart. As they spoke, I could feel tears swell in my eyes from their pain and the raw beauty of their experiences. Many had no inkling of their words' profound effect on me; they were unaware that I had traversed through my dark times. My journey, marked by love, profound loss, and the flickering light of hope, mirrored theirs in many ways.

One woman stood out in the dim light of the center as she shared her deeply personal struggles. Her voice trembled slightly, each word laced with emotion, yet an undeniable strength radiated from her. As she spoke, I felt a powerful connection forming that stirred memories and emotions I thought I had buried long ago. Her story resonated within me, echoing the silent battles I had faced—battles that had often felt too heavy to articulate.

What struck me the most was how she seemed unaware of her narrative's impact on me and others in the room. It was as if a more excellent, invisible force was weaving our experiences together, creating an unspoken bond of understanding that transcended the confines of language. Although she didn't know the specifics of my journey, I couldn't help but feel that the Lord recognized our shared pain and resilience.

When she concluded her story, I felt compelled to express my gratitude. "Thank you for bravely sharing your story with me," I said, my voice steady despite the emotions swirling inside me. A warm smile emerged on her face as she replied, "Thank you for listening." In that moment, I realized how powerful it is to share and receive stories and how, even in our struggles, we can find a thread of unity that connects us all. Isn't this how authentic connections are developed?

Being authentic in a relationship doesn't mean it is without its bumps and hurdles; it just means that both individuals are comfortable being themselves, expressing themselves freely, and being willing to put in the effort to foster a strong bond based on trust, respect, and shared interests.

Chapter Two

MEANINGFUL FRIENDSHIPS ARE BUILT

I believe by creating a nurturing and secure environment for our hearts, we foster the opportunity for deeper connections to take root and thrive. This space allows us to share our unique experiences, diverse thoughts, challenging struggles, and raw emotions. In turn, we invite others to share their narratives with us, creating an atmosphere of mutual understanding and trust. This exchange becomes a sacred bond, where each person's truth is honored and valued, enriching our relationships and collective journey.

"To those of us who believe that all of life is sacred, every crumb of bread and sip of wine is a Eucharist— a remembrance— a call to awareness of holiness right where we are."

I wholeheartedly agree with this sentiment. I invite you to embark on the journey of cultivating a genuine connection. One of the most valuable gifts you can offer in this is your full attention. Being present and actively engaging in our interactions can foster a deeper understanding and appreciation for one another. Your willingness to invest your time and focus can make a difference in building a meaningful relationship.

Have you ever considered how a chance encounter with someone you meet on your journey could turn into a pivotal moment? Each person you cross paths with has the potential to become a significant character in your narrative. Imagine the depth of meaningful friendships that could blossom through these interactions, enriching your experiences and shaping your perspective. As you navigate the twists and turns of life, the connections you forge may bring unforeseen joy and understanding, weaving together the fabric of your story with threads of shared laughter, challenges, and unforgettable moments.

When we fully and completely dedicate ourselves to another person, without any distractions, we offer the greatest gift we can provide: a heartfelt connection that allows us to bond on a deeper level. These connections unite individuals and foster meaningful friendships where none existed before.

Phoebe ELDER ALICIA WALKER

Fifteen years ago, I crossed paths with Alisha, affectionately known as Lisa, at the Consumer Product Safety Commission in Bethesda, MD. Although she worked on a different floor, our interactions were frequent, as I was a contractor serving as a FOIA Analyst, and my desk was strategically positioned near the entrance. Whenever Lisa visited a co-worker on the floor, I couldn't help but notice her striking stilettos, which she donned every single day without fail.

I had become well-known in the office, and my cubicle was a hub of activity. Colleagues would frequently stop by to say hello or wave as they hurried out the door. However, my social exchanges caught the ire of my cubicle mate, who grew increasingly frustrated with the constant interruptions. One afternoon, she erupted in a loud outburst over the cubicle wall, expressing her displeasure at what she perceived as my rudeness.

The situation quickly escalated when I decided to confront her by walking over to her doorway to inquire about the source of her distress. Her frustration turned into an argument, which led us to involve our supervisor to mediate the conflict, as she had reported me for being disruptive. Amidst this turmoil, Lisa, who had heard about the commotion, made a bold entrance into my cubicle without saying a word. In a dramatic gesture, she began removing her jewelry and slipping off her stilettos before praising God with an old-fashioned dance to distract me from the situation with my cubicle mate. Her actions reminded me to focus on the Lord instead of the conflict at hand, strengthening our shared beliefs in God and deepening our connection.

In that moment, Lisa embodied the essence of true friendship, ready to stand up for me against adversity. We forged a close bond that day, realizing how divine providence often sends the right people into our lives during moments of strife, even without a spoken word of support. Reflecting on that experience, I am grateful for the discernment that guided our paths to intersect, ultimately turning a frustrating encounter into a lasting friendship.

True friendships are marked by open communication and steadfast support, never by conflict. We often find ourselves laughing about the amusing moments we've shared, as they serve as a cherished reminder of who God is and how He consistently intercedes in our lives. Although I don't have the opportunity to speak with Lisa daily, I keep her in my thoughts and prayers regularly.

Whenever we gather, our laughter resonates so loudly that it catches my husband's attention, who often shakes his head with a playful grin, amused by our infectious joy. I cherish those spontaneous moments when, if I'm in her neighborhood, I might call to see if she's home for an unplanned visit. Even a simple drive-by, just for a warm hug and a shared smile, fills me with happiness before I continue on my way.

I can't express enough how much I appreciate this type of friendship. Lisa is not just a friend; she is genuinely my Sistah friend. We share a bond that allows us to talk about everything under the sun, and I trust her entirely with my thoughts and feelings. We've traveled together, enjoyed cozy pajama parties at the movies, and shared countless meals, often with crabs spread across the table, our laughter and stories flowing freely.

These moments define our connection, and I wouldn't trade this beautiful aspect of our relationship for anything. Our friendship is a treasure, and the bond is evident, bringing great joy into my life.

A deeply emotional moment arose when Lisa's son, Curtis, tragically passed away. She was faced with the unimaginable decision of donating his organs. One of the recipients was my husband Robert, who received Curtis's kidney after enduring the exhausting cycle of dialysis for five long years. The news of Lisa's loss hit me like a heavy wave, especially knowing that at that time, she was staying in a hotel—a temporary refuge since her home had caught fire just weeks earlier.

Without hesitation, I jumped into my truck, feeling a mix of urgency and concern, and made my way to the hotel where she was staying. I parked and walked towards her room, my heart heavy with empathy. I knocked gently on the door, and when it opened, I immediately stepped inside without waiting for an invitation.

The atmosphere was heavy with grief as I entered the room. Lisa was curled up under the covers, her body shaking with deep, heart-wrenching sobs that echoed the profound sorrow of a mother who had just lost her child. I didn't hesitate; I pulled back the covers, climbed into bed beside her, and held her tightly until her crying subsided.

In that delicate moment, words felt completely inadequate, mere whispers lost in the weight of the situation. I wrapped my arms around her, offering the comfort of my silent presence, anchoring her amidst the turbulent waves of her grief. The warmth of our shared silence enveloped us, serving as a soothing balm for the rawness of her pain. It was a poignant reminder that sometimes, in the face of unbearable loss, the most profound gift one can offer is unwavering support—a steadfast willingness to simply be there, side by side, sharing the heavy burden of sorrow with a friend in desperate need of comfort.

Whenever Lisa arrives at my home, she steps through the door with an air of warmth and familiarity, embracing me tightly before instinctively moving toward Robert. There, she gently lays her head against his stomach, seeking the reassuring presence of Curtis, the son she lovingly entrusted with a part of herself by donating a kidney. It's a ritual steeped in love and remembrance, a tangible connection to the life she fought so hard to preserve.

Lisa is Phoebe, our bright light—a truly remarkable soul whose unyielding spirit has transformed our lives in ways we couldn't have foreseen. With her infectious smile and radiant positivity, she creates an atmosphere filled with warmth and joy, effortlessly uplifting the spirits of those fortunate enough to be in her presence.

Her laughter is like music, soothing and invigorating, and we often find ourselves reflecting on how profoundly grateful we are for the abundant joy and grace she brings to our family every single day. Each moment spent with her is a beautiful testament to the power of resilience and love, capturing the essence of what it means to cherish one another.

Whether she is sharing her dreams, engaging in heartfelt conversations, or simply enjoying piles of crabs, her genuine kindness and unwavering support leave a lasting impact on our hearts. We hold her dear in our lives, grateful for the countless memories we've created together and the profound legacy of love and joy she has woven into the fabric of our family. Everyone needs a Phoebe like Lisa.

Chapter Three

InSight To Sistahhood

Caught in a moment of despair, you found yourself ready to give up. Even as your storm reached its peak, there she was, praying and interceding on your behalf. She may not have known all the circumstances or how deep your pain ran, but she recognized that you needed her support. So, she picked up the phone to hear your voice. Her encouraging words uplifted you when you answered: "Phoebe, girl, I've got your back!"

A *Sistah* is an invaluable gift to the heart, embodying the essence of friendship and serving as a spiritual companion. She is like a unique thread intricately woven into the fabric of our lives, enhancing the richness of our existence. When Sistahs unite and stand shoulder to shoulder, the strength we create is formidable—who could stand a realistic chance against us?

A Sistah acts as your mirror, reflecting your most authentic self-back to you and unveiling many possibilities for growth and transformation. She is your unwavering witness, perceiving you in moments of despair and joy and loving you unconditionally despite your flaws. She imparts wisdom and guidance as a teacher, helping you navigate life's challenges and reminding you of your worth. Her presence in your life is often why you find the strength to persevere.

While we may gather friends along our journey and occasionally encounter rivals, our Sistahs belong to a different realm of connection—integral to our being. She profoundly understands who you are; she is familiar with your faults and virtues, struggles and victories, conflicts and reconciliations, and the deepest longings of your heart.

You stand together, bound not just by shared experiences but also by an unbreakable bond forged under the sacred laws of Sistahhood. This camaraderie transcends mere friendship; it is a spiritual alliance that honors the individual and the collective, celebrating the power and magic that arise when Sistahs walk side by side through life.

In the heart of life's whirlwind, where chaos swirls around us like an unrelenting storm, there exists a quiet yet powerful force—a bond that transcends the boundaries of time and circumstance. In one such stormy moment, when I felt myself teetering on the brink of despair, I heard her voice cut through the cacophony like a radiant beacon, calling me back to a place of safety and belonging. *"Phoebe, girl, I've got your back!"* she exclaimed, her words resonating with a raw sincerity that wrapped around my fragile spirit like a warm embrace. Instantly, they ignited a flicker of hope, reminding me that I was not alone in my struggles.

Ah, what a priceless gift a Sistah truly is! She is much more than just a friend; she embodies the essence of Sistahhood, a divine spirit whose presence is intricately woven into the fabric of our lives. In those moments when the world's weight seems unbearable and the night feels interminable, her brilliant light illuminates the path ahead, guiding us through the darkest times. We stand as an unbreakable circle, shoulder to shoulder, united in a fierce alliance that dares to challenge the impossible and confront the obstacles that life throws our way. Who, in their right mind, would stand a realistic chance against us when we rise together as one—invincible, fierce, and unwavering in our resolve to support and uplift each other?

In her eyes, I glimpse the reflection of my highest self—the person I aspire to become. They are not just eyes but windows to a world of potential and hope. She holds up a mirror that reveals my deepest aspirations and dreams, encouraging me to look beyond the veil of fears that often cloud my vision. Whenever I falter or doubt myself, she reminds me of the immense strength within me—a strength that courses through my veins, passed down from generations of resilient women who have faced life's challenges with grace and tenacity. She becomes my unwavering witness, capturing the essence of my journey, both in moments of struggle and in times of triumph.

During my lowest moments, when uncertainty and despair threaten to overwhelm me, she stands steadfastly by my side. In my highest moments, when I soar and celebrate my achievements, she is the first to cheer me on, sharing in my joy. She is a true pillar of love and support, embodying a sense of comfort and understanding that is grounding and uplifting.

In her presence, I feel liberated to be vulnerable, to peel away the layers I often wear as armor, and to reveal my most authentic self. She intimately understands my flaws and virtues, my greatest catastrophes alongside my most cherished victories; she sees my life's intricate tapestry. Each shared secret reinforces our bond, every tear we shed together strengthens our connection, and every uncontrollable laugh intertwines our hearts in a profound and unbreakable way. In a world that can often feel isolating and cold, she is the rope that keeps me anchored to my sense of humanity—a lifeline that ensures I am never alone in my struggles, no matter how daunting they seem.

Sistahhood is not merely a matter of friendship but a profound and sacred bond forged through shared experiences, deep emotional connections, and an unwavering mutual understanding. Throughout our lives, we have navigated tumultuous storms that threatened to tear us apart and faced daunting battles against external forces that sought to erode the foundation of our relationship. Yet, through each challenge and heartache, we always emerge more vigorous, resilient, and fortified by our steadfast loyalty. Our connection is steeped in an incredible depth of understanding, guided by the sacred codes of Sistahhood that seem to be whispered into our souls by the universe itself.

In the face of adversity, whether a personal struggle or a shared challenge, we consistently find solace in one another's presence. This unwavering support proves time and again that love and loyalty can withstand even the fiercest tempests that life can throw our way.

Reflecting on a particularly pivotal moment, where her voice pierced through the fog of my despair, I realize how invaluable her presence is in my life. She embodies an essence of hope and courage that inspires me daily, reflecting all the beautiful qualities I sometimes struggle to see in myself. Together, in the complex dance of life, we navigate the ups and downs, creating a harmonious melody that resonates with laughter, heartfelt support, and a kind of love that nourishes our spirits and fuels our ambitions.

To my beloved Sistah, I want to express my eternal gratitude. In those moments when the storms rise, and the weight of the world feels unbearably heavy, your unwavering belief in my potential and your constant encouragement carry me forward. Together, we form an unyielding force. Together, we are truly unbreakable. Together, we will confront and rise above whatever challenges life places before us, for we are bound together by deep love—Sistahs at heart and allies for all of our lives.

We all may find ourselves caught in a tumultuous moment of life; you find yourself standing at the precipice, teetering on the edge, ready to let go of everything familiar. The storm within you churns violently, building to a deafening crescendo that threatens to drown out everything that once brought you comfort—hope, faith, and even the very breath in your lungs. When it feels like despair has stitched the darkest threads into the fabric of your existence, she appears—a radiant beacon cutting through the tempest with her unwavering light and unshakeable resolve. She may not know the depths of your anguish or the intricate web of your struggles, but what she does understand is your profound need, and in recognizing that need, she discovers her purpose.

She reaches out to you with a quick flick of her wrist and the simple sound of a tap on her phone screen. When your call connects, her voice slices through the chaos surrounding you, resonant and clear, enveloping you in warmth and reassurance. "Phoebe, girl, I've got your back!" Those words are like the sweetest salve gently applied to fresh wounds, wrapping you in a comforting embrace that transcends distance, time, and circumstance. In that instant, her unwavering faith transforms into your lifeline—an anchor amidst the storm.

Phoebe, a faithful Sistah, is nothing less than a precious gift to your heart, a steadfast friend to your divine spirit, and a thread intricately woven into the very fabric of existence itself. In a world that often feels isolating and lonely, when Sistahs stand shoulder to shoulder, it is as if the universe bows before the collective strength of your bond. Together, you possess an unshakeable power; who could stand a realistic chance against the two of you? She mirrors your soul beautifully, reflecting the essence of you and the limitless potential of who you could become. The realms of possibility stretch endlessly ahead of you, painted in vibrant colors that only she can reveal, illuminating paths you may never have imagined.

She is your unwavering witness, standing steadfast and resolute as life throws you between moments of unbridled triumph and heart-wrenching disaster. She sees you at your worst—when your insecurities and fears bubble to the surface—but loves you fiercely despite it all. Her heart is fully committed to your journey, embracing your myriad transformations without a hint of judgment. Over time, she has become your teacher, a source of unyielding strength, and the reason you persist through life's tumultuous waves. Friends may come and go, floating in and out of your life like passing clouds, and enemies may emerge from the shadows, fueled by envy or misunderstanding. But the Sistahs are here to stay, deeply rooted in an unwavering commitment marked by loyalty, love, and an unbreakable bond that withstands the test of time.

In every shared laugh and every tear that falls, she delves deeper into the layers of your being—discovering your imperfections, recognizing the gentle qualities illuminating your spirit, and understanding the devastating moments that almost shattered you. She celebrates the big and small victories that propelled you into the sky like a soaring bird. She knows your competitors, comprehends your deepest aspirations, and yet, with unwavering commitment, chooses to walk this journey alongside you, hand in hand, against the often-overwhelming complexities of a world that can feel too burdensome to navigate alone.

United by the sacred codes of Sistahhood, you share a profound understanding that this bond goes beyond simple friendship. It is a connection meticulously woven by divine intention, a promise of steadfast support and unconditional love that assures you—you are never genuinely navigating life's challenges by yourself. As the tides of life rise and fall, you realize that with every challenge faced and each moment of openness you embrace, you carefully craft a rich tapestry, interlacing threads of resilience, joy, and an enduring Sistahhood that cannot be broken.

And so, as you weather every storm and overcome each trial, keep this in mind: you have a Sistah who stands firm beside you. She is your anchor in tumultuous seas, your guiding voice of reason during moments of confusion, and your forever cheerleader who believes in you wholeheartedly. With her unwavering presence beside you, you can confront the world head-on, and against all odds, you will rise higher than you ever imagined.

Chapter Four

What Paul Says About Phoebe

Phoebe is a notable figure in the first-century Christian community, explicitly mentioned in the Bible in Romans 16:1-2 NIV:

> *I commend to you our sister Phoebe, a deacon of the church in Cenchreae. I ask you to receive her in the Lord in a way worthy of his people and to give her any help she may need from you, for she has been the benefactor of many people, including me.*

A prominent leader within the early Christian community in Cenchreae, a thriving seaport near Corinth. She played a vital role in the church as a trusted member and a benefactor who provided support and resources to many individuals. Among those she aided was the Apostle Paul, who recognized her contributions and influence.

Paul trusted Phoebe to deliver his letter to the Romans. Paul refers to her both as a servant and a deacon. He gives Phoebe a lot of honor and glory, thus paying due respect to her position within the church. Also, he calls her a "helper" of many people, showing that she was pretty engaged in helping others in their ministries. Paul calls on the Romans to extend due hospitality and help Phoebe, reminding them of her tremendous help to him and other believers.

What It Means

Beyond this introduction, these two verses offer key details regarding Phoebe's life and vocation. First, Paul calls her a

---

"deacon." Paul's words about Phoebe's official role in the church also refer to her character and ministry. This is consistent with the general view that women occupied essential roles in early Christianity, and how Paul talks about Phoebe suggests that she was a woman of high standing. In addition, it shows that, in Paul's view, she was a helpful partner in proclaiming the gospel, thus depicting how believers should treat each other with due courtesy and appreciation. The Greek word for "deacon" is *diakonos*, and it is elsewhere translated as "servant" or "minister." In his essay "What Can We Say About Phoebe?" J. David Miller argues that Paul's usage of *diakonos* in Romans 12 carries the notion of leadership. He writes, "Phoebe's description as *diakonos* includes the qualifying phrase 'of the congregation in Cenchreae.' This localization of Phoebe's position strongly suggests Paul had in mind a specific status rather than general comportment."

PHOEBE WHO?

The story of Phoebe is quite helpful for understanding the part of women in the church in the first century. Some critics believe that her status shows that women could have leadership positions in the church and the wider society. Others consider Phoebe an example of a Christian disciple because her commitment to helping people is an example of the love and life of Jesus Christ. In general, it is possible to state that her story contributes to recognizing women's roles in the early church and stresses the importance of women in ministry and mutual support.

The biblical figure of Phoebe teaches us the importance of offering heartfelt service to the Lord and the church. By using our God-given gifts, talents, and resources, we can demonstrate our genuine faith in Jesus. We are called to help whenever we see a need or an opportunity to serve.

Phoebe was part of a larger cohort of women who partnered closely with the Apostle Paul, women such as Chloe (1 Corinthians 1:11), Nympha (Colossians 4:15), Apphia (Philemon 2), Euodia and Syntyche (Philippians 4:2-3), and Junia (Romans 16:7). Sometimes Paul gets labeled as being "anti-women." Still, Phoebe and her Sistahs would surely testify otherwise.

Phoebe's home base is Cenchreae, a coastal town about five miles southeast of Corinth. From Paul's words in Romans 16, we know that there was a Christian church in Cenchreae and that Phoebe had some sort of significant role in the church's life.

The passage starts with Paul "commending" Phoebe to the Roman Christians, the letter's original recipients. Why would Paul feel the need to commend Phoebe to the Romans? One possible answer is that Phoebe carried the letter to Rome on Paul's behalf. Indeed, some believe that not only was Phoebe the letter carrier, but she also likely explained the letter to its first hearers. One scholar noted, "Phoebe carried under the folds of her robe the whole future of Christian theology."

Miller, Jeffrey D. "What Can We Say About Phoebe?" CBE *International*, Priscilla Papers, 2011, www.cbeinternational.org/resources/article/priscilla-papers/what-can-we-say-about-phoebe.

DIGGING DEEPER

Phoebe, as a Deacon and Benefactor

In Paul's letter to the Romans, when he speaks of Phoebe, he clearly describes her status within the church at Cenchreae. Phoebe is a leader, so Paul writes about her to the Romans. If the Romans knew some of Phoebe's actions, they would have paid more attention as she unfolded the scroll to read them the letter.

Paul also refers to Phoebe as a "benefactor." In the Greco-Roman world, benefactors, or patrons, funded various social enterprises. As a benefactor, Phoebe was a woman of some means who was generous with her support of others, Paul in particular. Theologian Marg Mowczko writes, "As well as being an important part of Roman society at all levels, patronage was also important in the church. Edwin Judge has remarked, 'Christianity was a movement sponsored by local patrons to their social dependents.'"

What's the significance of Paul commending Phoebe to the Romans by noting her status as a benefactor? Perhaps it testified to the integrity of her character. The Roman church should welcome this generous, committed, sacrificial woman into their community.

Chapter Five

SHE IS CALLED - WE ARE CALLED

How might Paul's description of Phoebe in Romans challenge us in the diverse contexts we encounter in today's world? Her titles not only highlight her significant role within the early Christian church but also encourage us to reflect on how we recognize and celebrate the contributions of women and other marginalized voices in our contexts. How can we embody the spirit of inclusion and service that Phoebe represents, and what does this mean for our personal interactions and the structures we engage with in our daily lives? Engaging with these questions can inspire us to foster environments that uplift and empower those who serve, regardless of gender or background.

One of her divine callings from God was to take an active role in leading the church and guiding God's people on their spiritual journey. This brings to mind a crucial question: "In what ways are you stepping up to lead within your church community?"

Reflecting on Paul's teachings and actions, how can we actively promote and celebrate the unique gifts and contributions of women in our church context? Additionally, consider the profound message in Mark 8:34-38: what does it mean to lose your life for the sake of the Gospel? How can you embrace self-sacrifice to more effectively serve and uplift the people of God, ensuring that your leadership not only inspires but also enriches their lives?

Phoebe played a vital role in the lives of those around her, including the Apostle Paul. We encounter countless individuals who are struggling, feeling lost, or experiencing hardship. Reflect on how Jesus might be calling you to step into the role of a benefactor for those in need. What tangible actions could you take to support them? Whether it's by offering your time to listen, providing financial assistance, or simply sharing words of encouragement, consider how your unique gifts and resources could contribute to healing and hope in the lives of others. What steps can you take to embody this spirit of generosity and compassion in your everyday interactions with other women?

Phoebe's name originates from the Greek language, meaning "shining" or "radiant." This beautiful etymology serves as a powerful reminder of the impact we can have through our actions. As we reflect on Phoebe's exemplary life, may we strive to embody her spirit by illuminating the lives of those around us with the light of Christ. Let us embrace a leadership style characterized by humility and service, alongside a generosity that mirrors Christ's own selflessness. In doing so, we can emulate Phoebe's legacy and inspire others to shine brightly in their own unique ways.

Chapter Six

THE GOD OF RELATIONSHIPS

The God we serve is a God of relationship, a God of community, and a God of love and trust. One word comes to mind as I reflect upon what true Sistahhood should embody - Authentic! Think about it. How many times have you thought to yourself how wonderful it would be to have a Sistah friend you could trust and would trust you in return? I have heard women say they do not trust women because they are fake, phony, and hypocritical.

AUTHENTIC MEANING

1. Not false or copied: genuine and original, as opposed to being a fake or reproduction
2. Trustworthy: shown to be genuine and trustworthy.

Yes! Sistahhood is built upon each Sistah's authenticity to create an atmosphere based absolutely on trust. For the most part, trusting someone with ourselves is challenging yet not unimaginable. A Sistahhood built upon trust is only established as each Sistah is willing to reveal more of herself, which ultimately promotes a deeper sense of one's security.

To be honest, I don't believe there is a woman who doesn't long for an authentic friendship where she can share her heart in a *"safe place"*—without being judged for her failures or bad decisions, past or future—yet she will be embraced, empowered, and lifted to soar again.

As I embrace God's calling for my life, I must acknowledge where I am now. I feel a deep hunger for genuine, honest communication. I desire a real bond with other women—a Sistahhood. I find it frustrating when many women wear a 'nice' or 'good girl' mask. Is it because they fear disapproval and/or rejection?

I want to be part of a Sistahhood that celebrates our strengths and supports each other in facing our weaknesses. I want to share light-hearted moments when I make mistakes. I want a group that inspires and pushes me to be my best. I hope for a community that celebrates our achievements and helps each other when we struggle, rather than staying in a victim mindset.

I want to join a Sistahhood where we can share everything about ourselves—our richness and poverty, our highs and lows, our love and losses, our strength and challenges. I am ready for this. Will you join me?

I was in a place where I wanted to trust and be trusted. However, I knew all too well the pain of genuinely opening oneself to another, only to be betrayed or belittled in the long run. And all though I understood this, a thought lingered in the back of my mind: "Was I willing to open the vault of my heart and become vulnerable again?"

We often feel overwhelmed by our emotions during stressful times. A friend we trusted has let us down, which has left us hurt. We struggle with the belief that we cannot trust anyone with our good and bad feelings. We've almost given up on finding these kinds of connections. Still, we wonder if we can find at least one trustworthy person.

Every day, we pretend to care and show our true selves to those who depend on us. They need our support to handle their struggles, but we also need to take care of ourselves. This cycle goes nowhere. We feel stuck, repeatedly experiencing the same emotions of hurt, anger, and resentment. We also deal with envy when we see other women in the relationships we want.

We feel sad thinking we might never find a close sisterhood that accepts and celebrates us for who we are. I don't want to pretend that I'm okay being alone and competing with others. I realize that the real competition is within myself. I ask myself, what can I offer to others?

Thinking about my life has made it harder for me to have real, genuine relationships. This worries me. I ask myself: How much have I missed by not connecting better with others? How many people reached out to me, and I did not respond? Have I been blocking my own way?

Authentic – There's that word again! The only way to truly connect with others is to be true to ourselves first. We need to open up, which can be especially complicated for women. I have several women in my life who are loving and honest in their relationships, but many layers remain unpeeled.

A QUESTION TO PONDER

Think about someone in your life whom you admire and want to learn from but are afraid to trust them. Remember, a true friend loves you all the time. (Proverbs 17:17).

> *A friend loves at all times, and a brother is born for a time of adversity.*

Chapter Seven

NOT EVERYONE WILL LIKE OR TOLERATE YOU

Dealing with human relationships can be challenging, especially when someone seems to hold a grudge against you or causes trouble in your life. However, it's important to understand that honesty can be a valuable gift. It shows us that not everyone shows their true selves behind a friendly appearance. The person who acts like an enemy might have become a good friend, but more often, those who seem friendly can reveal a darker side when the time is right.

Think about a colleague who seems supportive in public but secretly works against your projects when no one is watching. Or consider a person who says they are your closest friend but spreads harmful rumors to hurt your reputation. Also, think about a romantic partner who claims to care for you but often ignores your needs and goals. These situations remind us to pay attention to our relationships and value the few genuine connections that truly enhance our lives. By staying positive and resilient, you can learn important lessons from each experience, even the difficult ones.

Feeling disliked can deeply affect us, often leaving longer-lasting hurt than the presence of insincerity or dishonesty. Many people might change their behavior to fit into different social situations or to appear better to others. However, it's important to understand that someone acting in bad faith may not always mean to be harmful. This behavior often comes from their own insecurities or life experiences.

People who dislike you often hide a mean or selfish side of their character, which can reveal a more troubling aspect of their personality. They might act superior or distant, hiding their true intentions behind harassment or passive-aggressive behavior. Being disliked can create a toxic environment, making us doubt our worth or change who we are to fit in. This complex behavior highlights the need to approach social relationships with empathy and care.

Understanding the critical distinction between genuine and superficial interactions can empower you with the insight necessary to navigate and avoid negativity and toxic relationships. Remain vigilant for specific warning signs that may indicate insincerity:

Extravagant Compliments: Pay attention to exaggerated praise that feels excessive or forced. While compliments can be uplifting, those that seem disingenuous often serve as a facade to mask ulterior motives.

Gossip Patterns: Observe the dynamics of conversation within your social circle. If discussions frequently devolve into gossip, with a palpable atmosphere of mistrust, it can create a toxic environment that stifles authentic connections. This negativity can linger, much like a noxious fog that affects everyone present.

Passive-Aggressive Remarks: Be wary of comments cloaked in vague language yet sting with underlying hostility. These types of remarks can undermine your confidence and create an atmosphere of anxiety and uncertainty.

Recognizing these traits can unveil a duplicitous nature that often hides beneath a facade of friendliness. Trust your intuition when gauging the authenticity of those around you, and embrace the transformative power of genuine positivity.

Surround yourself with individuals who uplift you and inspire you to be your best self.

Building strong relationships with people who care about you is important for your mental and emotional health. These connections create a supportive environment where real friendships can grow. By fostering these relationships, you can handle life's challenges better and find strength and happiness along your journey.

DON'T BE TOLERATED

Many people say that we need tolerance to improve the world. However, I don't like the word "tolerance" because it can have negative effects on people over time. I wouldn't want anyone to feel they have to tolerate me. That is not a good feeling. I want to be accepted. Acceptance is different from tolerance. Acceptance means being open-minded and trying to understand each other. On the other hand, tolerance often feels like this: "I don't like you and probably never will, but since you are here, I will just ignore you."

If we want to improve our Sistahhood, we should aim for acceptance instead of just tolerance. Tolerance allows dislikes to continue. We can embrace people, communities, and ideas.

Often, we miss the mark. I've spent time with others and listened to various complaints, and after these conversations, I frequently felt uneasy. I want to emphasize that I have never shared anyone else's opinions about the people they were discussing. Instead of supporting the person, as encouraged in Galatians 6:1-10, we sometimes fall short.

> *"When you observe someone making a mistake or committing a wrongful act, it often involves the idea of*

gently correcting or guiding them back to the right path. This concept is commonly found in religious contexts, particularly in the Bible verse Galatians 6:1, which states, 'Brethren, if a man is overtaken in a fault, you who are spiritual should restore such a one in the spirit of meekness.'"

When I notice that I am having negative thoughts about someone or a situation, I take a moment to pause and reflect. During this time, I examine why I am feeling this way, and I often realize that my own biases and assumptions may be influencing my perspective. I understand that these internal factors can distort my judgment and lead to unnecessary negativity.

I also recognize that some situations are particularly challenging. Interacting with people can sometimes be difficult and may trigger some strong emotions. Despite this, I strive to balance my feelings with an awareness of the complexities of human behavior. By doing so, I am working to cultivate compassion and acceptance, even in tough situations.

"Can't we all just get along" is a phrase most commonly associated with Rodney King, who uttered it during a televised plea for peace following the 1992 Los Angeles riots after he was brutally beaten by police officers, captured on video, sparking widespread outrage; essentially asking for people to coexist peacefully despite their differences.

I also ask, why can't we find a way to coexist peacefully and harmoniously by setting aside our differences to foster understanding and compassion towards one another?

Chapter Eight

WILL YOU HELP ME UNPACK MY BAGS?

We've all gone into relationships pretending we are baggage-less. Who doesn't have baggage? It's about something other than how you unpack as it is important where you have stowed it. Don't get it twisted. We may have found ourselves seeking someone to help us 'unpack our luggage', but remember, you will need to help them unpack theirs.

Everyone we meet has their own experiences, challenges, and emotional baggage. Look for someone who appreciates you for who you are and can help you understand and deal with these complexities together. This journey can create deeper connections and personal growth as you both support each other in overcoming past struggles and looking forward to the future.

So, how do you unpack those issues? *One Item at a time.* Unpacking the issues has to do with your decisions regarding how to unpack. I remember wanting someone to hear me out, but I shared too much with the wrong person, which drove them away. Lesson learned: you can only unpack with someone willing to carry your baggage to the storage area. Sharing too soon will leave you open and vulnerable with nowhere to go. In other words, you are left standing with your mouth wide open, and the other person has left you feeling a little cray-cray. Now, why did I share that? That was not the right person.

UNPACKING

Most of us have shoved the unpacked bags under the basement stairs of our souls, and we dare not uncover them for fear of shame, judgment, and rejection.

How can we ever find true Sistahhood and genuine friendships if we are afraid to let someone help us unpack our emotional baggage? I understand that one must be willing to be unpacked in order to assist others in unpacking their bags. This process of unpacking requires a safe environment. Vulnerability arises as we all recognize that our burdens are too heavy, preventing us from achieving the depth of authentic friendship. If God desires truth within us and created us in His image, then we, too, must reach a point where unpacking our baggage becomes essential for growth in our relationships.

I have entered many relationships on a superficial level, often claiming that I had no emotional baggage. While I wanted to share my thoughts and feelings, I also approached these relationships with a lack of trust. Maintaining this superficial facade led me to shut down and retreat into my own corner of silence. By believing the lies I told myself, I built a barrier that made it difficult for others to connect with me. This situation impacted many areas of my life, including the way I carried myself, how I interacted with others, and most importantly, how I perceived these connections.

Our friendships are influenced by our personal histories and life experiences, both good and bad. If we have felt unloved or inadequate in the past, we may doubt our worth in relationships. These feelings can affect how we connect with others. We might protect ourselves by being cautious with our hearts or seeking approval from friends. Our experiences shape how we view trust, closeness, and the importance of friendship.

In some failed relationships, the outcome wasn't our fault, and we didn't deserve what happened. Looking back, we realize that our poor decisions and rushing into these relationships made us appear needy. Regardless of where our past wounds and scars originated, we can take responsibility for our actions and make changes now. Let's start fresh.

> *Your success in friendships depends on your willingness to UNPACK and finally get rid of the baggage.*

Are you ready to unpack the barriers of old friendships and embrace new Sistah friendships? Letting go of this baggage can be scary. It will require you to redefine some areas by becoming vulnerable.

Building strong connections with others can be difficult as we age. However, it is possible to achieve this transformation. This guide will share practical strategies for turning casual friendships into deeper relationships. We will focus on building closeness, improving communication, and creating shared experiences that strengthen your bonds with others. These methods will help you develop a more supportive and rewarding social life.

"How to Be a Friend" looks at the key parts of friendship, focusing on trust, respect, and open communication. True friendships grow from shared experiences and the support we give each other in tough times. It is also important to accept and understand our differences. To keep these friendships strong, we need to make a deliberate effort and engage with one another actively.

Reaching out and connecting with others is essential because it encourages openness and authenticity in our interactions. Friendships are dynamic; they evolve and change throughout our lives. This serves as a reminder to value our connections and actively work on building and maintaining them.

LET'S UNPACK

Our deepest fear is not that we are inadequate. Our deepest fear is that we are powerful beyond measure.

~ Marianne Williamson

> Drop what's holding you back. Lighten that load. Release your potential, and let's get connected.

Our past failed relationships do not define us. Yes, you may have made some mistakes and a few poor choices. However, keeping score of these does not lead to anything good. What is significant, though, is who you have become now.

Use your past mistakes as tools for learning and growth. Your challenges can shape you into the person you are meant to be, creating a true Sistahhood experience. For this reason, you must intentionally let go of old baggage. Remember, the enemy does not want authentic Sistahhoods to form. He will try to convince you that all women are the same, that you don't need to share your experiences, and he will feed you the biggest lie: remember how deeply you were hurt the last time you trusted someone?

It's important to first reject the misconception that anyone can be completely self-sufficient. In fact, it is the Father's will that we engage in sincere, caring, trustworthy, safe, empowering, supportive, and authentic fellowship as we navigate through life together.

Chapter Nine

OUR FUTURE IS FULL OF POSSIBILITIES

Possibilities are *created*
Possibilities are *invented*
Possibilities are *refined*
Possibilities are *acted on*

Break through the barriers of limited thinking and explore the possibilities life has to offer! Find inspiration and allow yourself to dream again, embracing all God intends for you in your friendships.

What new possibilities can you create for your new Sistah friend? Focus on making memories that bring joy, appreciation, and acceptance.

Your past may have significantly influenced how you experience the present moment. Embrace the now and be excited about the new friendship that awaits you.

It's time to move forward and shape your life from this day on. Recognize your worth, because you are stronger, wiser, and aware of the life you want to live and share with your new Sistah friend.

SISTAHHOOD

Many people assess their happiness based on the quality of their relationships. No one relates perfectly, and even those who relate well can recognize that they may need to improve from time to time. The same principle applies to Sistahhoods.

In our Sistahhood connections, we create an environment that nurtures personal growth and deep intimacy. This is accomplished through the time and effort we dedicate to cultivating meaningful relationships. We should approach each other with openness, honesty, and authenticity, as these qualities form the foundation of true Sistahhood.

We often hide our true selves, showing only parts that do not reflect our real feelings or experiences. If we want our authentic Sistahhood to grow and thrive, we need to create a welcoming and supportive space. This way, every woman can feel empowered to express herself freely.

In this supportive environment, we can offer each other grace, love, and unwavering support. This allows us to grow both individually and collectively. By cherishing and prioritizing these values, we can deepen our connections and strengthen our bonds, creating a powerful Sistahhood that uplifts and inspires us all.

> *Genuine Sistah-hood is about relationships. Most people value their close personal relationships in Sistahhood more than anything else in life.*

We want to create a space where Sistahs can find the love they seek. This Sistahhood will be more than just sharing warm feelings; it will help us raise our expectations and understand that each person plays a role in the relationship. This requires real strength, especially as we support each other over the years. Imagine committing to this for the long term. As we build our community of Sistahhood, we can all feel connected to one another. Whether with a Sistah, a friend, or with God, we naturally desire this level of closeness because it's what we were made for. We all want to experience true Sistahhood in our lives. Our hearts long for this connection. We can all improve our ability to relate to each other and communicate with love.

Chapter Ten

A Friend Is a Treasure

> *Friends come, Friends go, but a true friend is there to watch you grow.*

"When you find a friend, you find a treasure."

"Friendship is one of God's greatest gifts. It brings beauty and joy to our lives. Friends help us through boring times and tough moments."

True and lasting friendships can happen suddenly. In **1 Samuel 18:1–3 (NLT)**, *after David talked with Saul, he met Jonathan, the king's son. They instantly connected because Jonathan loved David. Saul kept David with him from that day and did not let him go home. Jonathan made a strong promise to David because he loved him as much as he loved himself.*

True Sistah friends

What does a true Sistah friendship look like?

Let's break it down:

1.
Sistah friends Love Sacrificially

> John 15:13 (NIV): *Greater love has no one than this, that he lay down his life for his friends.*

Jesus is the best example of a true friend. His love for us is selfless and sacrificial. He showed this through miraculous healings and washing His disciples' feet, and ultimately giving

His life on the Cross. As Sistah friends develop their friendship, both must understand this idea—each should be ready to support the other when in need.

If we choose our friends based only on what they can do for us, we may miss out on genuine friendship. The Bible verse Philippians 2:3 advises us, *"Do nothing out of selfish ambition or vain conceit, but in humility consider others better than yourselves."* When you put your friend's needs before your own, you start to love like Jesus. This way, you may find a true friend.

2.
SISTAH FRIENDS ACCEPT UNCONDITIONALLY

Proverbs 17:17 (NIV): *A friend loves at all times, and a brother is born for adversity.*

We celebrate the value of true friendships among women. These friendships help us accept each other's weaknesses and imperfections. This is important because everyone has flaws. Instead of judging or looking down on our friends for their shortcomings, we should stand by them and help them to become stronger.

We will struggle to make friends if we get easily offended or hold onto anger. No one is perfect. We all make mistakes sometimes. If we look honestly at ourselves, we can see that we also share some blame when problems arise in a friendship. A good friend asks for forgiveness quickly and is also ready to forgive. A good friend speaks the truth with kindness so that their friend does not stumble.

Luke 6:39 (NLT) *"Can one blind person lead another? Won't they both fall into a ditch?*

3.
SISTAH FRIENDS TRUST COMPLETELY

Proverbs 18:24 (NIV) *A man of many companions may come to ruin, but a friend sticks closer than a brother.*

This proverb shows that a true Sistah friend is someone you can trust. However, it also points out an important fact: we can only fully trust a few loyal friends. Trusting someone too quickly can lead to disappointment, so be careful about relying on someone who is just a casual friend. In time, our real Sistah friends will prove trustworthy by staying close.

4.
SISTAH FRIENDS KEEP HEALTHY BOUNDARIES

1 Corinthians 13:4 (NIV): *Love is patient, love is kind. It does not envy, it does not boast, it is not proud.*

It is important to set healthy boundaries as friendships develop. If you feel overwhelmed in a friendship, something is wrong. If you feel taken advantage of, that's also a sign that something is off. Recognizing what someone needs and giving them space shows a healthy relationship. We should never allow a friend to interfere with our relationship with our spouse if we are married. A true Sistah friend will respect your need to maintain other relationships and will not intrude.

5.
SISTAH FRIENDS GIVE MUTUAL EDIFICATION

Proverbs 27:6 (NIV): *Wounds from a friend can be trusted, but an enemy multiplies kisses.*

A true friend cares about your well-being and growth. They will give you honest feedback or constructive criticism, even when it's difficult to hear. This comes from a strong, trustworthy relationship where both feel safe and valued. Their goal is not to hurt you but to help you improve and become a better version of yourself. They show that they care about your journey and success.

True friendships help us grow emotionally, spiritually, and physically. Sistah friends enjoy being together because being in each other's company feels good. We offer strength, encouragement, and love. We talk, cry, and listen to each other. Sometimes, we also need to share hard truths that our Sistah friend needs to hear. This trust and acceptance allow us to speak honestly while being kind. I believe Proverbs 27:17 means, "As iron sharpens iron, so one man sharpens another."

Work on the traits mentioned to strengthen your friendships. Don't worry if you don't have many close friends.

True Sistah friendships are special and can take time to develop. Stay open to finding a great friend and remember that Sistah friends can come from unexpected places.

Many people, even those without many friends, understand that having close relationships, or Sistahhood, is important. When they consider what they value most, many say, "The people I truly love." Our greatest happiness comes from our connections with others. We need these relationships— material things cannot replace them. This is because not everything can love us back. We all want to love and be loved; it's in our nature. We are meant to connect with others, share with them, and receive from them through Sistahhood. Sharing life with others is a key part of our purpose. Friendships are gifts we allow ourselves to accept. Some people find this easy, while others struggle with it.

We can strengthen our friendships with other women. Building healthy relationships is both a skill and knowledge. While you can't just read to create strong bonds, exploring this topic together can help you gain valuable insights.

Chapter Eleven
WHY SOME MAY FEEL "DISCONNECTED"

As an evangelist, I meet many young and old people who want stronger and more meaningful relationships with other women. Many feel lonely and disconnected. Although we rely on technology like high-speed Internet, instant messaging, email, and cell phones daily, many people seem to have less meaningful connections. It feels like technology is working against us.

Many people say they have no time. When did you last write a letter or even a simple note by hand? A handwritten note feels more personal than a typed message or an email. This way of communicating is richer and more genuine. You might ask, "Who has time for handwritten notes these days?" This shows our real issue: we often say we lack time. But do we really not have time, or do we not make the time? There has been a big change in how we communicate. We have swapped depth and meaning for speed and convenience.

Some people feel disconnected in their relationships because they don't understand true friendship. They might have learned hidden messages or beliefs from their upbringing, social surroundings, or past experiences. These messages can create obstacles that stop them from recognizing and valuing real connections. As a result, they may hesitate to fully engage in friendships, which can keep them from enjoying meaningful relationships with amazing people who could enhance their lives. Recognizing and overcoming these hidden beliefs is important to build genuine and fulfilling friendships.

There is an important message that has been shared among women who have experienced pain. This message highlights the need to change harmful words and beliefs that make us feel alone and cut off from the caring relationships we want. To connect with others and build meaningful relationships, we must face and let go of the stories that keep us apart. We need to explore the deeper parts of ourselves, finding the valuable qualities hidden inside us. This exploration can happen only when we accept and show our true selves, allowing our real identities to shine and helping us create genuine connections with others.

Some people think we have a problem with interpersonal relationships, especially with Sistahhood. Here's a quick test: write down the first names or initials of anyone, including family members, with whom you can talk about "important matters" privately and healthily. If your list has no names, we must address this issue.

We all need at least 1-2 people to have "vault conversations." In a vault session, we enter into a conversation, close the door, say what needs to be said, and then come out and securely lock the door behind us. Nothing can get in or out unless it is unlocked and opened.

Phoebe BISHOP LIZA R. HICKMAN

Occasionally, I need a serious and confidential conversation, so I reach out to my dear Sistah friend, Bishop Liza Hickman. I am always mindful not to take advantage of our friendship because I deeply respect her time and the demands of her role. Whenever she was available for a private chat, my phone would ring with her call.

As soon as I pick up, I'm greeted by the unmistakable sound of a large door creaking open, reminiscent of an unlocked heavy vault. Bishop Liza playfully mimics the sound of locks clicking into place, and then she joyfully declares, "The door is closed and locked!" We share a laugh, but beneath the lighthearted banter, I can genuinely feel her care and concern radiating through the phone. It's a reassuring reminder that our conversations are safe spaces filled with trust and understanding.

The experience of feeling disconnected impacts more than just our Sistahhood. How often have we considered ending a relationship due to a misunderstanding? Often, the real issue lies in a misunderstanding of genuine intimacy. Many people today seem confused about what true intimacy means, frequently equating it solely with sex.

Intimacy involves profoundly connecting with another person—two individuals sharing their inner selves. Recognizing that our relationships will vary in intensity and depth is essential. We should never pressure a Sistah friend to share information she may not be ready to disclose. Instead, we should continue fostering a safe, comfortable, and inviting atmosphere. In time, hearts will open, and deeper connections can develop.

Where has the genuine sense of Sistahhood gone? Why do our friendships often lack the depth of true intimacy? It's possible that we have fallen into the trap of relying on superficial connections or unhealthy relational patterns, which only serve to heighten our feelings of isolation and deepen our loneliness. Additionally, there may be an underlying fear of vulnerability—an anxiety about being exposed or perceived differently by our Sistah friends—that holds us back from forming closer bonds.

In contrast, my Sistah friendship with Bishop Liza Hickman stands as a testament to unwavering companionship over the years. For nearly four decades, she has consistently exemplified what it means to be a steadfast friend. Every time I visit Atlanta, we make it a point to take long drives together, just the two of us, to share quality time and create lasting memories. These moments are not only about conversation; they provide a sanctuary for genuine connection and mutual understanding. I feel incredibly blessed to have Bishop Liza in my life, as her presence enriches my journey with support, love, and authenticity.

Successful relationships blend the intricate elements of art and science. Every individual has unique gifts, talents, and temperaments—this represents the "science" behind our connections. Yet, developing and refining interpersonal skills are equally crucial, embodying the "art" of forming deep bonds. I firmly believe that the beautiful journey of Sistahhood unfolds a wealth of opportunities for personal growth, allowing us to explore the depths of our shared experiences, nurture our strengths, and embrace our differences.

WHAT IS SISTAHHOOD?

What does it mean to be a Sistah? People come into our lives in different ways. Some are acquaintances—people we've met but don't know well. We may talk to them, but it's not enough to call it a true Sistahhood. We might think of these people as "casual Sistahs," "buddies," or "companions." While we may spend time with them, real Sistahhood involves a more profound connection than these relationships often lack. I'm not saying the "buddy" connection isn't essential; it differs from Sistahhood.

We all know what true Sistahhood means. A "Sistah" is someone close to me—someone I trust and feel a sense of harmony with. This person is willing to show their true self, revealing their scars and wounds. Sistahs often connect through shared activities or similar values that shape how they see the world.

What is the core of Sistahhood? Is it mainly the sisters' love for each other, or is it about the loyalty they share? Is Sistahhood built on shared interests, or is it more about how well their personalities match?

What is the role of character and virtue in friendships? Do you need to be a "real" woman to be a good friend? How you answer this question reveals your ideas about Sistahhood. I believe that character and strength are important for true Sistahhood. While I agree with this, I also think that a good Sistah friend can help us improve the flaws we bring to our relationship. As we show our true selves, our character flaws and weaknesses might become visible. If our goal is authentic Sistahhood, this is where Romans 15:1-2 is important.

> *"Those of us who are strong should support the weak and not seek to please ourselves. Each of us ought to care for our neighbors' good, building them up."*

Sistahhood is more than just a label; it represents an intense way of connecting. It's a bond that changes friends into Sistahs. This change happens intentionally, not just because of shared interests or situations. What brings these Sistahs together is their deep care for each other's lives, well-being, and experiences.

This connection is more than just friendship. It means engaging with each other personally and meaningfully, where everyone can be their true self. By choosing to be Sistah friends, we build relationships based on trust, openness, and vulnerability. We share parts of our lives that we might not share with anyone else, trusting that our Sistah friends will keep our secrets and struggles safe and handle them with care and compassion.

This relationship creates a safe space to be our true selves, away from how others may see us. While many people might know me by my looks, my Sistah friends truly understand my heart and soul. They see my happiness, fears, and dreams, providing rare and valuable support. This is how Sistahhood becomes a meaningful commitment to care for one another, forming a strong and fulfilling bond.

As Sistahhood grows, significant changes start to happen. First, you will feel a sense of responsibility for each other. This doesn't have to be overwhelming. It simply means your relationship will go beyond casual friendships. Those with a closer sisterly bond will naturally take on more responsibility for one another than casual friends do.

When we take care of each other, we improve our relationships. I feel safe knowing she will keep my secrets when I share something important with my close friend. This trust is a sign of our strong bond.

A true friend understands how personal my feelings are and is dedicated to keeping my private thoughts safe. By guarding my secrets, she makes sure that my feelings are respected. This strengthens our friendship and builds the mutual trust that is essential to it.

To Sum It Up

- *A Sistah friendship is being there to encourage through good and bad times.*
- *A Sistah friendship is authentic and provides personal security.*
- *A Sistah friendship is not judgmental or condemning.*
- *A Sistah friendship is about sharing dreams and achieving goals together.*
- *A Sistah friendship is about aspiring each other to reach greater heights and exceed expectations.*
- *A Sistah friendship is about counting on others and being counted on to make a difference.*
- *A Sistah friendship is one of the greatest treasures ever found.*
- *A Sistah friendship is an experience of a lifetime.*
- *A Sistah friendship is God's desire for His daughters.*

Chapter Twelve

TOXICITY IN RELATIONSHIPS

Are you surrounded by someone who drains your energy and enthusiasm, leaving you feeling depleted? Are you in a relationship where constant criticism undermines your confidence and self-worth? Are you experiencing emotional manipulation that makes you hesitate to express your true feelings? If you answered yes to any of these questions, it's clear that you're in a toxic relationship.

Toxic relationships can occur in friendships, family, or romantic partnerships. These harmful connections can drain your happiness, increase your anxiety, and lower your quality of life. The first important step to improving your emotional health is to recognize that you are in a harmful situation.

It's important to surround yourself with people who uplift and support you. Look for relationships based on respect, support, and positivity. By nurturing these healthy connections, you can improve your self-esteem, happiness, and overall outlook on life. Remember, you deserve relationships that inspire you and help your well-being. Take control of your connections and embrace the positivity you deserve.

- Ponder your relationships with the people in your life. Identify which relationships are positive ones. Positive relationships leave you feeling refreshed, loved, and secure.
- Identify toxic relationships by analyzing the relationship and asking questions in the steps below.

- Ask yourself these two questions: Does this person lift or bring you down? Do I feel better or worse about myself after I'm with this person? Being around toxic people can be very draining, leaving you with a less-than-pleasant feeling. In addition, toxic relationships can damage your health. Migraines, stomach aches, depression, stress, and tension can result from a toxic relationship.

- Consider whether the person shares your values. When values differ radically, the relationship can become a battle zone, which can create stress.

- Ask yourself if you feel safe around this person. Is the person physically or emotionally harmful? Abuse is part of a toxic relationship, whether physical, verbal, or emotional.

- Consider whether the relationship is a positive or negative one. Some toxic relationships appear favorable, but upon examination, you will find that the relationship centers on the other person and isn't a balanced, give-and-take relationship. This type of relationship is based upon control and is unhealthy for you, and you need not remain in such a relationship.

- After you've identified a toxic relationship, take steps to minimize your time with toxic people and lessen or eliminate their impact on your life.

SIGNS OF A DANGEROUS RELATIONSHIP

If you ever feel threatened in a relationship, it's crucial to trust your instincts and take the time to reassess the situation. Unhealthy relationships can lead to various forms of abuse, which may be both overt and subtle. These abuses can take several forms: psychological, emotional, sexual, financial, or physical.

Psychological abuse often involves manipulation and constant criticism aimed at undermining your confidence and creating anxiety. Emotional abuse may manifest as a lack of support, rejection, or withholding of affection, all of which can severely impact your self-esteem. Sexual abuse includes any unwanted sexual advances or coercion that disregards your boundaries. Financial abuse occurs when one partner exerts control over finances, making you dependent or restricting your access to essential resources. Physical abuse, which is often recognized as the most overt form, involves any act of violence or aggression.

Abusive behavior can include tactics such as intimidation, threats, or attempts to isolate you from supportive friends and family, creating a feeling of entrapment. Recognizing these warning signs is crucial, especially if you've experienced relationship issues, as they can indicate potential danger.

It's important to remember that there is no justification for any form of abuse. Whether the behavior is driven by drugs, alcohol, stress, or anger, abusive actions are always a conscious choice made by the abuser. You have every right to be in a loving, respectful, and safe relationship. Taking steps to prioritize your well-being is a powerful and courageous decision. Don't hesitate to seek support; it's a vital step toward reclaiming your confidence and ensuring your safety.

WARNINGS FROM LOVED ONES

Recognizing the warning signs of a dangerous relationship is important, even if it's hard when you're emotionally involved.

A key sign to watch is when family, friends, or others express concern about your partner's behavior. If they describe your partner as controlling, self-centered, or possessive, these are serious red flags you should not ignore.

People may hesitate to share their feelings because they care about you or are worried about your relationship. However, it's vital to listen if multiple people share similar concerns about how your partner treats you or mention specific incidents that worry them. Their insights can help you notice harmful behavior patterns you might miss.

Trusting these insights is vital. By acknowledging and addressing these warnings, you empower yourself to make choices that prioritize your well-being and happiness. Taking action is an important step to building a healthy and supportive relationship.

IDENTIFY YOUR FEELINGS

If you often avoid disagreeing with a friend because you fear their anger, this is a sign of an unhealthy relationship. Healthy relationships allow for open communication and sharing of different opinions without fear of backlash.

If you constantly feel like you must tiptoe around your friend to protect their feelings or avoid feeling guilty, it's time to recognize that this is not a supportive relationship. You deserve to express your thoughts and feelings freely without worrying about extreme reactions.

It is important to avoid being pushed into activities or decisions that make you uncomfortable. Your choices matter, and you should always feel free to set your boundaries. If someone consistently tries to manipulate or pressure you, it is essential to confront this behavior directly. Always prioritize your mental health and happiness. You have the right to build relationships that respect your independence and well-being.

BAD BEHAVIOR

Pay close attention to how the person you are with treats you and others, both in public and private. Look carefully at their words, tone, and actions. If they often belittle, humiliate, or embarrass you—whether in front of others or when you are alone—this is a sign of emotional abuse and can harm your relationship.

Also, talk to your trusted friends and family about your relationship. They may have seen concerning behaviors or patterns that you should consider. Even if they didn't speak up because they wanted you to be happy, their views can help you better understand your relationship. Trust your instincts and take action to protect your well-being.

WHO'S RESPONSIBLE?

A person who often blames others for their disappointments, failures, or problems does not take personal responsibility and lacks emotional maturity. If this person tries to convince you that the success of the relationship depends only on your willingness to change, this is a big warning sign of an unhealthy

In a healthy relationship, both partners recognize their flaws and weaknesses. This helps build mutual respect and support. Open communication happens when both people take responsibility for their actions, leading to personal growth.

If you keep trying to change to make this person happy—thinking it will fix the relationship—it's time to step back and think about the situation. Consider whether the issues come from your behavior or if they are due to the other person not facing their own problems. A clear look at the real issues will help you make good choices about the relationship's future. You deserve a partnership that is based on equality and shared responsibility.

HOW TO END A TOXIC RELATIONSHIP

Managing a toxic relationship can be tricky, especially with someone you've known for a long time. If someone in your life is harming your emotional and mental well-being, it's crucial to take action to address and possibly end the toxicity.

First, identify the toxic traits you might encounter. Recognizing these traits will help you handle the situation better. The criticizer blames and belittles others, which can hurt self-esteem. The complainer focuses only on the negatives, ignoring the good and creating a negative atmosphere. The blamer shifts responsibility onto others, making communication hard and tense.

The drainer takes away your energy with constant negativity and emotional demands, leaving you tired after every conversation. The shamer humiliates or mocks you, leading to feelings of inadequacy. The gossiper spreads rumors and shares your private matters, damaging trust in your relationship.

Once you spot these toxic traits, consider how they affect your life and well-being. Set clear boundaries and express your feelings confidently. Remember, prioritizing your well-being is not just important; it's your right. Distancing yourself from toxic people is necessary for a healthier, happier life. You deserve relationships that lift and empower you.

List the people and their toxic behaviors in your life. Then, examine each relationship. A person may be toxic if your relationship has more negatives than positives.

Consider the cost of cutting ties with a toxic person. If it's your spouse, boss, or parent, you might think ending the relationship could cause too much loss. Instead, think of ways to change how you respond to their behavior, which might change their behavior, too.

Know your worth. Your body language often shows how you really feel.

Calmly confront the toxic person. Share your honesty with them. Explain what bothers you about their behavior and how it makes you feel. Ask if they are willing to change. If not, think about cutting all ties with them.

Traits of An Unhealthy Friendship

Thinking about the friendships in my favorite TV shows made me question how realistic they really are. Shows like Friends and Sex in the City show friendships that many of us desire. These friendships last for years, survive tough times, and involve regular conversations, often daily. The characters are honest with each other, even when it's difficult. They create the feeling of an ideal friendship.

Building deep and meaningful friendships requires much effort, commitment, and dedication from everyone involved. Like in romantic relationships, personal problems can affect friendships, leading to misunderstandings and conflict.

To keep a strong friendship, it's important to communicate openly. Address concerns before they turn into bigger issues. This means being clear about your feelings and really listening to your friends. By working through conflicts and caring for the relationship, friends can create a supportive space where both can thrive and grow together. We all know that no one is perfect. While we look for specific qualities in friends, we also need to recognize when a friendship is unhealthy. We should focus on relationships that uplift and support us.

1. JEALOUSY

It's normal for everyone to feel envious at times. We might envy a friend's job, relationship, or ability to have children when we can't. However, when envy turns into resentment or jealousy, it becomes a problem. If your friend can't move past their feelings to be happy for you during your good times, it may show that their issues are more important to them than your friendship.
Following Jesus and not comparing oneself to others.

> John 21:20-22 NIV - *Peter turned and saw that the disciple whom Jesus loved was following them. (This was the one who had leaned back against Jesus at the supper and had said, "Lord, who is going to betray you?") When Peter saw him, he asked, "Lord, what about him?" Jesus answered, "If I want him to remain alive until I return, what is that to you? You must follow me."*

The disciples sat around the table for the Last Supper, an important event. John, the youngest disciple, was so close to Jesus that he could lean against Him, showing their special bond. In John 21, Jesus and John had a deep conversation about John's challenges in serving Him. This talk highlighted

John's future responsibilities and the glory that would come from his faithfulness.

As their conversation continued, Peter looked at John with urgency and curiosity. He asked Jesus for His plan for him since they expected a challenging journey ahead. Peter wanted reassurance and wondered if John would go through similar struggles.

Jesus responded to Peter with a calm demeanor, yet His words carried a firm weight. He encouraged Peter to direct his attention inward and concentrate on his own journey, stating, "Mind your own business." This profound response served as a powerful reminder of the importance of individual responsibility. It emphasized the necessity for each person to commit fully to their own mission without becoming distracted by the paths of others. By urging Peter to focus on his own calling, Jesus highlighted the significance of personal accountability and the dedication required to fulfill one's purpose in life.

THEN THE RUMORS STARTED

Why did Peter notice this? Why was he worried about Jesus's relationship with John? This shows how jealousy can suddenly rise in our hearts and minds.

Focusing too much on what others are doing can distract us from our lives. Jealousy, envy, and comparing ourselves to others can trap us and keep us stuck.

Jealousy is intense. Our thoughts, beliefs, and values shape what makes us feel jealous.

Negative thoughts lead to feelings of insecurity, fear, and anxiety about losing something. We may feel we deserve what others have, especially if they got it before us. This feeling of entitlement can fuel our jealousy. Certain personality traits also influence what triggers our jealousy.

Why did Peter notice this? Why was he worried about Jesus's relationship with John? This shows how jealousy can suddenly rise in our hearts and minds.

Focusing too much on what others are doing can distract us from our lives. Jealousy and envy can trap us and keep us stuck.

Jealousy can be intense. Our thoughts, beliefs, and values shape what triggers our jealousy. Negative thoughts cause feelings of insecurity, fear, and anxiety about losing something. We might feel we deserve what others have, especially if they received it before us. This sense of entitlement can increase our jealousy. Certain personality traits also affect what triggers our feelings.

2. DESTRUCTIVE FEEDBACK AND COMMUNICATION

Honesty is essential for healthy relationships. It builds trust and openness between people. However, it's important to communicate honesty respectfully and kindly; otherwise, it can be harmful. Good communication means sharing the truth while considering how our words affect others.

Giving honest feedback <u>should</u> help each other grow rather than bring each other down. If someone often makes comments that upset you or lower your confidence, it shows an unhealthy dynamic. These comments do not aim to help and can cause emotional pain, weakening your relationship. It is important to set boundaries and focus on positive conversations that benefit both people. Healthy communication should support and encourage both partners, creating an environment where everyone can succeed.

3. Selfishness

Sometimes, your Sistah friend's needs will come before yours; other times, it will be the opposite. It's important to recognize that a friendship can become unhealthy if your friend's needs are always prioritized over yours. A good friendship is based on mutual support and care, where both people feel valued and heard. This balance needs active listening, shared responsibilities, and consistent support during hard times. True friendship grows through mutual respect and understanding, creating a strong bond that helps both people thrive.

4. Lack of Reciprocation

Are you always the one reaching out or making plans with your friend? It's important to understand how your friendship works. Some people find it hard to make the first move, but if you're always the one taking the lead, it's time to think about this. Doing this constantly can be tiring and might make you feel unappreciated in the friendship. You deserve to feel important. It's crucial that your efforts are matched and that the friendship feels balanced. Take a moment to think about whether this friendship is fulfilling your needs.

5. Incessant Negativity

The saying goes that misery prefers to keep the company it has; people typically find consolation in the fact that they are not alone in their misfortunes. It is also heartening to know that we have people we can turn to and who will listen to us when we are going through a tough time. However, if the only thing that you and your friend have in common is that you both like to complain and wallow in negativity, then this can be the foundation of a very harmful friendship. It can create a negative environment where the two of you will continue to console each other on your misfortunes rather than encourage each other to grow. As much as possible, friendships are supposed to be a help and a source of positive influence and encouragement in our lives. Healthier friendship also provides sympathy during hard times, but at the same time, it encourages each of the participants to work on themselves and to appreciate each other's achievements. This way, you will be able to maintain a healthy and positive relationship between the two friends to help them grow.

6. JUDGMENT

Judgment in a friendship can be detrimental to your spirit, undermine your self-confidence, and create doubt in the trust you have for each other. A true friend is someone who wholeheartedly accepts your decisions, respects your views, and understands your needs without imposing their opinions as the only "right" way to think or act. Healthy friendships celebrate individuality; just because something works for your friend doesn't mean it's the best choice for you. It's essential that both of you feel free to express your true selves without fear of judgment.

If you see any troubling behaviors in your friendship, it's important to address your concerns honestly. Start a conversation with your friend about how you feel. Avoid placing blame. By talking about the issues together, you can identify the root causes and find solutions to fix any problems in your relationship. This effort can strengthen your bond and lead to a better understanding of each other's perspectives. Remember, open communication is a key to building a strong and supportive friendship.

Chapter Thirteen

CONNECTING AND DISCONNECTING

Friendship is one of the most meaningful parts of our lives. Research shows that good friendships improve our physical and emotional health. However, many women feel pressured to keep unfulfilling friendships. They often stay in these relationships out of loyalty, fear, or guilt. This pressure can create more stress than ending the friendship would.

Friendship is the connection between two people at any time. It is unrealistic to expect that your closest friend at one point will always be the one you want by your side as you go through life. If a good friendship later becomes less enjoyable, it doesn't take away from the positive experiences you had together. Sometimes, friendships fade as people grow and change; it doesn't mean someone did something wrong.

FRIENDSHIPS CAN BE COMPLICATED TOO

It's no surprise that friendships can be just as complicated as they are in TV shows and movies, just like romantic relationships. Most conflicts are caused by misunderstandings so it is necessary to consider what you have done in order to contribute to the conflict. In some cases, friendships can end on a bad note. It can be difficult to know what you should do when both people have different opinions. There isn't as much definition with respect to how to end a friendship as there is for divorce in marriage. It can make you feel emotional and uncertain of whether you should end it and how to go about doing it. Though there are no specific guidelines, there are some clear indicators of the deteriorating friendship. You don't like yourself when you're with her. You might feel mean, passive-aggressive, or even angry. Maybe you feel competitive, resentful, or jealous, feelings you don't have with other friends. You may need to accept that you don't want the best for her. If this is true, what does friendship really mean?

1) Your friend might be causing you to act in harmful ways. You may be overcommitting, lying more often, being less patient with your kids, or feeling stuck in your creativity and values. You could also notice that your job or grades are in trouble, or you might start to question your marriage in ways you hadn't before. There are many ways a friend can negatively influence you.

2) The friendship feels unbalanced. You might notice a lack of give-and-take. Maybe she often borrows your things and doesn't give them back, or you've cooked for her so many times that it feels like you're just a cook. On the other hand, she might try to do a lot for you, but you realize you don't want to return the favor. Either way, the important balance in a deep friendship is missing.

3) You often have negative thoughts about your friend. You might make fun of them in your mind, and it's not kind. You may feel superior to them, which makes them annoying. You don't share laughs with them anymore, and you don't seem to enjoy their company.

5) Your friend doesn't seem to understand you. She might get your actions wrong or make you feel embarrassed about how late you sleep, what you wear, or how you cook. You may feel

unappreciated and put down, which can make you hide your true self. Or, out of annoyance, you might show off your "flaws" just to irritate her. Either way, this isn't unconditional love.

Can a friendship that has faced tough times be repaired? It's likely, but it depends on whether the problems are seen as isolated incidents or if they reveal deeper issues. Consider what your friendship is built on. If it's based on respect, trust, and shared experiences, then there may be hope for mending it. Also, think about whether you have doubts about several friendships or just this one.

A careful examination that reveals more negative characteristics than positive indicators require understanding that not every friendship needs to stand the test of time. What people fail to realize is that in any friendship, there is real kindness, understanding, and respect—elements that makeup truly meaningful relationships. Understanding this can assist you in dealing with the difficulties of friends

Chapter Fourteen

FRIENDSHIPS WILL EITHER FEED YOU OR BLEED YOU

KNOW WHEN TO LET GO

You've got to know when to hold'em
Know when to fold'em
Know when to walk away
And know when to run,
You never count your money
When you're sittin' at the table
There'd be time enough for countin'
When the dealin' is done

Songwriter: Don Schlitz

It's no surprise that most people enter our lives through social connections or chance encounters rather than through personal choice. These connections often depend on our circumstances or fate. Sometimes, it's important to reconsider where we invest our energy, especially since our situations can change. To live authentically, we must be honest about our relationships. This means acknowledging the reality of a relationship and not overlooking the negative aspects that harm us. In friendships, we should not tolerate toxicity or negativity that is detrimental to our well-being.

Relationships that form out of convenience—such as those at work, in the neighborhood, or through children's activities—tend to be fragile. When significant events occur, like moving or changes in life circumstances, these relationships are likely to change as well.

It is important for relationships to evolve when circumstances change. Such changes can prompt us to re-evaluate our connections and gain a clearer understanding of the true nature of our relationships. We can begin to see the strengths and weaknesses of our bonds, prompting us to ask whether they can withstand the changes or if they only function well within their original context. These realizations can be enlightening, helping us to grasp the true depth of our feelings.

When we recognize that a friendship is harmful, it may be necessary to create some distance. This realization can be challenging and may lead to feelings of uncertainty in our lives. However, practicing mindfulness requires us to reflect on how we invest our emotional energy. Spending time in a stagnant friendship can drain our energy and hinder our personal growth. In such situations, it might be in your best interest to distance yourself and seek out new connections that offer healthier support and a stronger sense of belonging. This shift can foster a more positive social environment and contribute to a more fulfilling life.

Chapter Fifteen

CAN YOU HANDLE TRUTH

Selecting friends is often a matter of the qualities they possess and what they are like as people along with the chemistry that exists between you. However own personal feelings of loyalty and support that these friends provide me in a way as I walk the walk of life is what really brings home deep feelings of love towards them. Their solace and support make them feel good about themselves and support their identity, which is something that we can all relate to. The shared support that we provide for one another only builds on our relationships and creates very important relationships that help with our growth as people.

Phoebe ELDER JOAN CARR-MILLER

I have a dear friend, Elder Joan Carr-Miller, with whom I have shared a friendship for over twenty-one years. Our bond has weathered the ups and downs of life. This one particular day stands out vividly in my memory. We were enjoying a leisurely lunch together when a thought from a sermon delivered by our Bishop Darnell Leach earlier popped into my mind. He encouraged us to explore the depth of our relationships by asking friends why they wanted to be friends. Feeling brave, I decided to put this into practice. I asked Joan, *"Why do you want to be my friend?"*

Her response completely took me by surprise. Without a moment's hesitation, she looked me straight in the eyes, her expression sincere yet unsettling, and said, "I don't." The abruptness of her reply hit me like a punch to the gut. I was so stunned that I turned on my heels and walked away, leaving her standing on the corner, likely reflecting on the impact of her words.

At that moment, I felt a wave of confusion and hurt wash over me; I wasn't ready to confront her feelings' full-blown, raw truth. I distanced myself from her for the next few days, not speaking to her as I processed the conversation and its emotions.

Eventually, we reunited, and she revealed her surprising response. She explained that she had been struggling with unresolved pain from past female friendships that had left her feeling jaded. When I asked her that question, it forcibly reopened those old wounds, tearing the bandage clean off her heart. This confrontation compelled her to reflect on her feelings about our friendship and the layers of trust and vulnerability that come with it. She said, "I liked you a little, but I trusted you none."

As time has passed, our friendship has evolved into something incredibly special. Today, there is virtually nothing we don't share; our bond has deepened to an extraordinary level. In fact, during a particularly challenging time when she was undergoing chemotherapy, she even joked, looking at me with a smile, that if we were any closer, we might as well be married. That moment was a testament to how far we've come, and I couldn't be more grateful for her presence in my life. Thank God for Jesus, who has blessed our friendship and helped us heal together.

Phoebe PASTOR CHANTELLE ELLIS-POOLE

There is a friend I met at a conference and bonded with within an instant. It was evident that this person would walk alongside me in true Sistah friendship. It took me a moment to connect deeper because all I could think about were my bad choices in past relationships. Lord, I want this one to work.

During one of our shared meals, I casually mentioned to Pastor Chantell Ellis that she was quickly becoming one of my closest friends. She turned to me with a playful glint in her eye and quipped, "You don't have any friends?" In that moment, I realized I had revealed a vulnerable side of myself. Unfamiliar with her lighthearted sense of humor, I instinctively turned my face away, exclaiming, "Oh no, she didn't... LOL."

From that point on, our conversation deepened, and although she did most of the sharing, her openness encouraged me to take a leap of vulnerability as well. As I began to open up, I noticed our authentic friendship blossoming in unexpected and profoundly fulfilling ways. A perfect example of this was when she took the time to drive over to celebrate my 55th birthday, even after a long day of preaching. I could see how tired she was, yet she chose to be there, and we ended up staying at the restaurant until nearly closing time, reveling in each other's company.

Since then, there have been countless moments that have solidified my belief that she is truly a Sistah friend—one whom I cherish dearly. It's often the small gestures and shared experiences that keep our connection strong. When I experience moments of doubt about the strength of our friendship, I reflect on these memories—those moments that remind me of her unwavering support. Having had no previous template for what it means to be a true friend, I feel incredibly fortunate to have her as a mentor in friendship. I strive to express just how special she is to me and make it a priority to share my appreciation for her presence in my life.

When people are asked, "What gives meaning to your life?" My Sistah friendships are correct at the top of the list. The dance of friendship is like no other. Sometimes, they will lead, and then sometimes, you will. We hear the same music of authenticity, which deepens our relationship and, therefore, allows us to remain faithful to who we have been called to be in this season of friendship.

MIRROR, MIRROR: THE TRUTH ABOUT BEST FRIENDS

If closeness forms the basis of friendship, then it is reasonable to assume that your best friend would be someone with whom you enjoy supersized intimacy. This intimacy goes "beyond the call of duty" of expectation. If we suffer an emergency – real or imagined – and need to talk, we expect our best friend to drop everything and race to our side or just be there to listen.

We select our friends based on the positive impact they have on our self-esteem and sense of self. I have an unending desire for identity support. There is no better example of connected friendships than those formed at a life-altering event.

BUILT TO LAST: HOW TO STAY FRIENDS

Our notion of what makes a good friendship changes, but our capacity to maintain one does. It's a reality; we know what being and having friends means. After we graduate from college and go our separate ways—

> Fundamental behaviors are needed to maintain the bond in the "best" friendships, and these behaviors hold true whether we're 17 or 90.

launching our careers, getting married, having children, getting divorced, caring for aging parents—we're often unable to muster the time and energy to maintain friendships we profess to value. Like anything else, remaining friends with someone requires a little effort. To be at the forefront, we must show up and be present.

Communication facilitates the first two vital behaviors: self-disclosure and supportiveness, both necessary for intimacy. We must be willing to extend ourselves, share our lives with our friends, and keep them abreast of what's happening to us. Likewise, we need to listen to them and offer support.

The third essential ingredient in a friendship is interaction. You need to write, call, or visit your friends. Find the nearest Starbucks and take some time to catch up. It doesn't matter what specific activity you choose; what's important is that you interact.

The most elusive behavior necessary for maintaining friendships is being active. The intimacy that allows a friendship to thrive must be enjoyable. The more positive we feel about it, the more energy we invest to keep it alive.

THE MAKING OF A TRUE SISTAH FRIEND!

I reflect on what true friendship means, especially when it comes to having a Sistah friend. I cherish my Sistahs and long for unity, love, respect, and honor to flourish among the women of God. Unfortunately, many women have shared feelings similar to mine, often rooted in past hurts or rejections. Nevertheless, this is a crucial moment for the daughters of Abraham to embrace healing so that we can love, honor, and support our Sistahs as we are meant to do. Jesus said in John 13:35 (NIV),

> *"By this, everyone will know you are my disciples if you love one another."*

If I truly care about my Sistah friends, I will support her wholeheartedly. I understand that some relationships may not have the deep connection I yearn for. However, this doesn't mean that I am not supportive, or that they are not supportive of me—it simply indicates that we struggle to trust each other on a deeper level. Unfortunately, this is a common issue among many women. We need to be open and willing to share our feelings with a Sistah. I have seen that building this trust is indeed possible.

For those who didn't have older sisters when they were young, sister-friends are like the big sisters you never had. Building our sisterhood will take time. We may annoy one another at times, but that's okay. It's important for everyone to keep trying and to stay open so that our genuine friendships can develop.

In our conversations, we may want to share certain things with one another, but we can't expect to know everything about each other right away. As our relationships grow, it will become easier to establish deeper connections as trust is built. So, try to relax and don't think that it's either all or nothing in terms of our friendships.

QUESTIONS TO PONDER

- Are you ready to be honest and honest to build real Sistahoods?

- What does Sistahhood look like to you? How can you make sure others can find you and walk with you in real friendship??

- What keeps you from revealing yourself to your Sistah friend is fear.

- What makes you worthy of someone's trust is the Sistah friend that you are, someone who can handle heart, secrets, and uncertainties.

Chapter Sixteen

IT MIGHT START WITH FORGIVENESS

Forgiveness is a powerful tool that can make you feel free and make a significant difference. It is not about the person who hurt you; rather, it is a crucial step in healing your heart and mind. Furthermore, forgiveness helps release resentment and pain.

This form of forgiveness originates from a compassionate part of yourself that desires healing. It allows you to find peace and well-being by acknowledging that in order to grow and heal, you must forgive those who have caused you pain or disappointment.

God promises, "If you feel empty inside, I will fill that space with My presence so you won't have to return to that painful place." When you present your struggles and heartaches to God, He will heal your deepest wounds as you rise from your brokenness. He can make each hurt within you whole if you allow Him in.

You are in my heart, and I want you to know that I understand what you are going through. Jesus is ready to assist you if you allow Him. He is teaching us important lessons about forgiveness. He said, "If you can let go of anger when people apologize to you, you will find a sense of peace within." By practicing forgiveness, you will be able to heal and experience that peace once again. Trust that Jesus will work everything out if you let Him.

While sitting quietly with your heart, you will discover forgiveness that transforms painful memories into lingering shadows. The words "I forgive you" free you to move on. This process reduces your anxiety, decreases your sadness, and allows you to let go of the heavy burdens you've been carrying.

It is essential to forgive the person who caused you pain, but it is even more critical if you are the one suffering. You find yourself at a crossroads, grappling with mixed emotions as you confront what has taken away your sense of self. Living through your father's abuse offers the opportunity to understand how to reclaim what feels lost and to free yourself from the heavy weight of hatred.

Don't hold onto the pain or remain bitter. While it's true that both parents have their issues, they are often unstable due to their personal experiences. Forgiveness does not mean forgetting; instead, it is a process of healing and reducing the pain you feel.

Holding onto unforgiveness is like harboring a destructive cancer within yourself, gradually consuming your emotional and mental well-being. There may be people in your life—friends, family, or acquaintances—who have wronged you in ways that linger and fester. It's important to understand that your journey toward forgiveness doesn't depend on whether they seek your forgiveness or acknowledge your actions. Instead, it is a powerful act of self-liberation. By choosing to let go of your grievances, you take a significant step toward healing.

Remember, forgiveness is a gift you give to yourself, allowing you to reclaim your peace and move forward unburdened by the weight of resentment. Forgive those who were not there for you when you needed support. This act of forgiveness benefits you and helps you overcome the anger that holds you back.

Most importantly, remember to forgive yourself. It is natural to feel angry and rejected; you have every right to be upset about what you didn't receive. However, holding onto that anger will keep you feeling like a victim.

Now is the time to release your anger, acknowledge your hurt, and begin healing.

An Initial Thought — Where It Started

You may have longed for your mother or father's love, a natural desire we all experience. When you meet them, allow those memories to surface, but try not to feel overwhelmed. At times, you may experience a sharp pain as their presence reminds you of the love you wished for and the love you never received. I understand that this can be painful. In those moments of hurt, remember the Lord's words: "I will fill that emptiness with myself, and you won't have to go back there."

I have always felt a strong desire for my mother's love, an ache that has lasted over 30 years. It seemed like there was a significant gap between us as if a wall was preventing me from achieving the deep connection I craved. Instead of feeling warm and close, our relationship often felt shallow and left me unfulfilled. I longed for her hugs that made me feel safe, her bright smiles that lifted my spirits, and that comforting embrace that made me feel valued. Unfortunately, those moments felt just out of reach, like a dream slipping away every time I tried to hold on.

As time went on, I began to notice a growing resentment in my mother's behavior toward me. This feeling was unsettling and left me confused. I couldn't understand why she seemed to withhold her affection. Her eyes, which could sparkle with joy, often appeared troubled. Not knowing the reason behind her behavior made it difficult for me to cope, leaving me feeling lonely and perplexed.

A Bitter Moment

One evening, while I was in the shower, I found comfort in prayer. With a heavy heart, I began to pray to the Lord, asking for help with my difficult relationship with my mother. I cried as I shared my pain, hoping for clarity and comfort. In that quiet moment, I felt a gentle whisper within me—a soft prompt that touched my soul.

The Lord whispered a profound truth to my heart: my mother could not give what she herself had not received. This realization struck me like a light bulb illuminating a dark room, dispelling my confusion and revealing the details of her past. I contemplated the love she may have longed for but never found, along with the challenges that had left their marks on her spirit.

Once I embraced this new way of thinking, I experienced a transformation in both my heart and mind. His Word became clear to me, changing my perspective. I realized that my mother was more than just the source of my pain and disappointment. This was an opportunity to see her as a complex individual rather than merely my mother, prompting me to try to understand her life. At that moment, I recognized her not only as a mother but also as a woman—a person with her struggles and unexpressed feelings who deserves compassion. Just one Word from the Lord changed my entire relationship with my mother.

What a beautiful belief! God spreads love everywhere. When you share your burdens—your painful memories, unmet needs, and wounds—with the Lord, you invite Him to be your safe space. The Lord will heal your pain and revive the parts of your soul that have suffered for too long. Healing can begin in the areas we think are unforgivable.

Speak your healing into existence. Let go of the grip that your pain has on your heart. Accept your current situation and move toward the new life waiting for you. Remember, you are loved, heard, and valued more than any pain, shame, or disappointment.

This is your journey. Each step you take toward forgiveness brings you closer to freedom. Every struggle with your pain helps you discover that freedom. Jesus is always there, welcoming you to reach your full potential—as a child, as a daughter, and ultimately, as a child of God.

You are not alone. Every step you take toward forgiveness brings you closer to peace, and every moment you confront your pain opens new opportunities for healing. Jesus invites you to be your true self: a daughter seeking a father and, above all, a beloved child of God.

You are on the brink of transformation! The power of forgiveness is here to support you. When healing begins, it brings an incredible sense of relief. If you can, ask the Lord to help you forgive someone. Prayer can be a vital first step toward healing and restoring relationships. This can be particularly challenging if you've been hurt by someone, as holding onto anger can feel more familiar than letting it go.

We all need forgiveness. It's easier to forgive others when we recognize that we also require forgiveness ourselves. Colossians 3:13 states:

"Forgive one another if any of you has a grievance against someone. Forgive as the Lord forgave you."

As you seek forgiveness in a relationship, let's not struggle to forgive yourself.

PRAYER FOR YOURSELF

Lord, I know that You have forgiven me. Thank You for Your unconditional love and grace. I repent and desire to overcome these feelings, I want to forgive. Father, please help me forgive myself. Erase my guilt and create a clean heart within me. Amen.

IF YOU ARE ANGRY WITH GOD

Lord, I admit that I am upset with You because of _____.

Help me to see things from Your perspective. I trust that You are a good God who always has my best interests at heart. Forgive me for carrying this disappointment. Heal me and restore my spirit. Amen.

TO FORGIVE OTHERS

Lord, _____ has hurt me. Though I may not understand why this has happened, I trust that You desire for me to forgive _____. Help me to comprehend the motivations behind _____ actions. Help me to fully release all burdens of hurt and un-forgiveness. Amen.

Chapter Seventeen
WAYS TO BE A GOOD FRIEND

Today, we can easily access information and connect with others globally. Yet many of us feel more disconnected, lonely, and isolated than ever. Social media lets us meet potential friends, but these connections often lack the depth needed for real friendships.

While technology makes our lives simpler and saves us time, it can also make us busier. This constant rush fills our to-do lists and reduces our patience. We can quickly "like" a post online, but we often find developing and maintaining deeper friendships hard.

In the *Sistahs In The City Ministry*, we believe "No woman should walk alone." Unfortunately, many women still feel alone. We work to create support groups for single moms in churches and encourage them to come together. Our main goal is to help these women form friendships that promote personal growth and a fulfilling life. Sadly, we often receive messages from women who feel lonely, without friends, isolated, and hopeless.

WE DO NEED EACH OTHER

We are made to have relationships with each other, and building these connections takes effort. We don't just say we want to be healthier; we watch what we eat and exercise to reach that goal. We also don't simply wish to build wealth; we track our spending, make a budget, and work hard to pay off debt. In the same way, we can't just say we want friends or feel lonely. We must be proactive in being good friends, creating meaningful connections, and nurturing both old and new relationships.

HERE ARE A FEW TIPS TO HELP:

LET IT GO: The relationship is more important than being right. Conflict will inevitably arise in any relationship—whether with a friend, coworker, parent, or child. At times, you may feel treated unfairly. Your friend might say something hurtful, handle a situation poorly, or act unjustly. However, the key is to let go of the need to be correct or validated. If the friendship matters to you, choose to set aside your grievances. Forgive quickly and often; you will need that understanding to help sustain your friendship.

BE HONEST: When someone asks for your advice, respond truthfully. If she wants to know how a dress looks and doesn't suit her body shape, express your thoughts kindly and honestly. Commit to being open and sincere if she inquires about a new boyfriend, job offers, or a book idea. Good friends provide honest feedback, helping each other grow and improve. Remember, it's also important to be a friend who can accept honesty in return.

AGREE TO DISAGREE: Disagreement is allowed. It is pretty standard to have differences in opinions on various issues. As much as you may have some common interests, every individual has his or her perspective in society, which is shaped by his or her experiences. This can sometimes lead to different points of view. However, it is important to handle interpersonal conflict positively and consider the other person's point of view, even if you disagree.

Practice genuine listening behavior. Turn off your phone and avoid thoughts about future responses or other distractions entering your mind. Focus on being present in the moment. Pay close attention to what your friend is saying. The simplest and most impactful way to support your friend may be by listening attentively and helping them feel heard, as this makes a real difference.

MAKE TIME FOR WHAT MATTERS. Be intentional in your actions. Act purposefully. Our daily routines include obligations such as family obligations and duties at work and in ministry. To keep friendships strong, actively nurture them. Engage in activities like sending messages, writing birthday letters, organizing meetups, or inviting friends for dinner. Building and sustaining friendships is quite difficult when you fail to nudge them up the ladder of concern in your scheme of things.

AVOID BEING OVERLY NEEDY. In friendships, as it can quickly harm the relationship. This includes constantly wanting to talk, visit, seek support, or have someone by your side all the time. It's perfectly fine to need support occasionally, but try not to place anyone on a pedestal.

Friendships should prioritize growth, laughter, wise advice, and enjoyment. We shouldn't depend on friends as our primary source of strength, hope, and purpose; that role belongs to our Savior. Friends often have busy lives with family commitments, and work can be challenging. It's essential to let friendships develop naturally without needing daily conversations or frequent check-ins. A healthy friendship allows both individuals to adapt to each other's schedules.

LAUGH FREELY and show your happiness, even if it tears your eyes. Watch a feel-good movie that makes you smile and laugh. Tell your favorite childhood stories that remind you of happy times, and share those funny, awkward moments that make you groan but still bring a smile. Remember, laughter is more than just a response; it's a potent medicine for the spirit, lifting your mood and helping you connect with others. Enjoy the joy from real laughter, and cherish the moments that make life special.

LET GO OF OFFENSE, bitterness, and anger. If we want to build strong connections with our sisters in Christ, we must not take offense easily. People who quickly take offense often struggle to keep friendships. It can be hard to be around those who are easily upset. If we react with anger and hold onto bitterness, we can't expect to have many friends. If you find this difficult, make a commitment to work on it, and you will see your friendships grow.

BE SELFLESS. Think about how you can help her. Relationships have good times and bad times. Sometimes, you will do most of the serving, and other times she will. There will be moments when you feel busy, emotional, or stressed, and you might need her support. At other times, you will be able to give support. You can bake a cake, babysit her kids for free, cook dinner, wash her car, clean her house, or surprise her with a kind act.

BEING FAITHFUL is important in friendship. Be the kind of friend who speaks kindly about others, whether they are present or not. Be honest, dependable, and a friend who stays during tough times. When problems come up—and they will—stay and work through them. Don't walk away at the first sign of trouble. People who have lasting friendships know that loyalty, along with determination and strength, is key to making those relationships work.

We want friends who will sit with us when we feel too sad to get up. We need friends who will help us when we're sick.

Friends who will take care of our kids when we've had a tough week. And friends who will drive us to chemotherapy if we have cancer.

BE AN ENCOURAGER. Lift each other up. Remember that "iron sharpens iron." When your friend leaves lunch with you, think about how she feels. Does she feel uplifted and encouraged or exhausted? Look for ways to praise her gifts and talents. Find chances to encourage her strengths. Offer wise advice guided by the Holy Spirit. Aim to be the kind of friend that others want to be with.

Sometimes, you will need encouragement too, and that's okay. Life can be tough, and you can't always be the one helping others. Still, it's important to make an effort to support those around you. If you focus on negative thoughts, it will be harder to keep your friendships. Try to spread positivity and hope wherever you go.

Chapter Eighteen

WHY RELATIONSHIP MAY CHANGE

Have you ever thought about why some friendships fade over time? Life can take unexpected turns, which may create distance even between close friends as we go through different stages in life. Changes like new jobs, moving to a different place, or family responsibilities can slowly weaken our once-valued connections.

Friendships can fade for various reasons, such as growing apart in interests or major life changes like marriage or becoming a parent. Learning how to keep these important connections strong as life changes is important. By understanding these issues and using thoughtful strategies, you can help preserve meaningful relationships and ensure they last, even as life evolves.

MAJOR LIFE SHIFTS - Big life changes, like getting married, starting a new job, or having a baby, can change our priorities and how we spend our time. These events can be emotionally and physically tough, leaving us with little time for friendships that used to be important. If we don't try to stay in touch, it's common for friends to drift away during these times. Keeping communication open, doing activities together, and planning regular meetings can help maintain friendships despite these life changes.

RELOCATION AND DISTANCE - Moving to a new city may make staying close to friends and family harder. Instead of daily chats, people often rely on occasional phone calls and texts. Over time, this can weaken those relationships. Without shared experiences like spontaneous meetups or coffee dates, connections can fade. Adjusting to new schedules and environments can also be tough, leading to feelings of distance. It's important to think about ways to nurture and maintain those relationships, even from afar.

CHANGING VALUES AND INTERESTS - As you go through life, your values, interests, and priorities change. This can lead to differences between you and your long-time friends. The activities and shared passions that once brought you joy may start to feel less important. Conversations that used to flow easily might become awkward or dull. These gradual changes in your life can create emotional distance, making your once-strong connections feel strained. Over time, what was a vibrant bond may weaken, and you may find yourself looking for new friendships that resonate more deeply with who you are becoming.

DEMANDING RESPONSIBILITIES - Responsibilities such as managing a demanding workload, caring for family members, or overseeing household tasks often consume the majority of our time and energy, leaving little opportunity for social interaction. The relentless pace of daily obligations can push the emotional and logistical investment needed to maintain friendships to the background of our priorities. As a result, even friendships that once felt significant and vibrant can quietly diminish over time without deliberate nurturing and communication. It's easy to overlook the importance of spending quality time with friends amidst the chaos of adult life, yet this connection is crucial for helping us recharge and find balance in our increasingly hectic schedules. If we fail to carve out moments for social engagement, we risk losing the very bonds that enrich our lives, which can lead to isolation and a sense of disconnection from those we care about most.

NEGLECTING COMMUNICATION - It is important to communicate frequently to build strong relationships. If we ignore small gestures of care over time, we can create distance between ourselves and others. Each missed chance for conversation adds up and can weaken the relationship. We often overlook how important these small actions are for keeping relationships healthy. By being attentive to others' needs and encouraging open communication, we can reduce the strain caused by neglecting one another.

BROKEN TRUST - A breach of trust, shown through dishonesty or betrayal, can seriously harm a relationship. Trust is essential for any meaningful connection, as it provides security and confidence between people. It's very hard to repair the relationship once trust is broken—whether by deceit, broken promises, or infidelity. The emotional wounds from such betrayals often last long, causing ongoing doubts and insecurities. As a result, many relationships struggle to survive after losing trust, and many do not recover from these deep effects. Rebuilding trust is challenging and requires time, open communication, and a shared commitment to healing, which not everyone can manage successfully.

SHIFTING SOCIAL CIRCLES - It's common for long-standing friendships to weaken as we form new relationships at work or in other social circles. Our desire to connect with new people and learn their stories requires our attention and energy, which can leave little time to nurture our older friendships. As a result, we may unconsciously neglect the needs of these longstanding relationships, leading to their deterioration.

These changes often happen naturally and without conscious awareness, causing us to develop emotional distance from friends with whom we once shared many memories. This unintentional drifting can evoke nostalgia as we reminisce about the great times and deep conversations with those friends. The absence of these connections creates a longing to recapture the comfort and support we once enjoyed, underscoring the importance of maintaining our historical friendships while pursuing new opportunities.

TECHNOLOGY REPLACING PERSONAL CONNECTION - Technology offers unique ways to connect with others but can also harm the quality and depth of personal relationships. Modern individuals often prefer text messaging, social media, and video conferencing to stay in touch with friends rather than engaging in face-to-face conversations. This reliance on digital communication tends to result in relationships built on shallow interactions instead of genuine connections. Although these exchanges happen frequently, they lack the heart and trust that come from sharing meaningful experiences and creating unforgettable memories while supporting each other through challenges. This dependence on digital communication can weaken the bonds of friendship, making them fragile and less resilient when facing life's complexities.

BE THE CHANGE YOU WANT TO SEE
START WITH YOUR RELATIONSHIPS

To bring about real, positive change in your life and improve your interactions with others, start by changing certain aspects of your behavior within your current relationships. First, take the initiative to adopt the qualities you often want to see in others. Practice kindness, respect, and understanding as core principles. When you consistently display these values, you set a powerful example for others to follow.

It's important to remember that communication is key. Listen to others, express gratitude, and share your thoughts and feelings—talk! These conscious actions will help establish a respectful and supportive atmosphere, leading to deeper and more satisfying connections.

YOU BE THE CHANGE

If we could change ourselves, the tendencies in the world would also change. A person's character influences their attitude towards the world and, in turn, the world's attitude towards them. This principle is especially true in relationships. Improving yourself rather than trying to change someone else to enhance the relationship is more beneficial. True transformation in relationships starts with small individual changes instead of dramatic actions. Each day presents a new opportunity for one person to choose to bring positivity into their life. You don't need the approval or attention of others; what you truly desire are meaningful interactions with those around you.

To initiate this change, begin by looking inward. Pay attention to your choice of words, tone, and body language. Every interaction is an opportunity, and with each action, you have the power to reshape your relationships. Treating others with kindness, respect, and genuine curiosity creates a ripple effect that extends to everyone you encounter.

As you embrace this journey, remember that the power to create change is in your hands. You don't have to wait for others to change their actions or attitudes; you can spark a new way of interacting simply by living out the values you hold dear. With each thoughtful gesture and act of consideration, you are building a legacy of kindness and respect that will resonate throughout every aspect of your life.

You must first change yourself to bring about change in your personal life and relationships. All significant changes start with you, and you can set an example for others. Accept personal development because you can create a better life for yourself and your loved ones through action. There is a world waiting for your leadership, and all you must do is move ahead confidently.

Your actions serve as a model for others. If you want respect, give it genuinely. If you want empathy, offer it freely. Every interaction is a chance to express your values. Use this influence with confidence. You are not just a participant in your relationships; you can spark change. By showing the qualities, you want to see in others, you take the first step. Don't wait for others to change; be the example you wish to see. This way, change becomes not just possible but unavoidable.

LEAD BY EXAMPLE

Focus on improving yourself. Please don't wait for others to change their behavior or attitude. Take charge of your personal development. Think about your actions and habits, and work on becoming the partner you want to be. This journey includes building emotional intelligence, communicating effectively, and showing empathy. By setting a positive example and growing yourself, you will enhance your relationships and create a healthier and more fulfilling connection with your partner.

Through your actions, show the behaviors you want in your relationships, like being supportive, communicative, and understanding.

Positive changes in your relationships can affect other parts of your life. Relationships are a small part of life, and good changes in them can spread outward.

HOW TO APPLY THESE CONCEPTS

IDENTIFY WHAT YOU WANT TO CHANGE. Think about how you want your relationships to improve through better communication, more respect, or greater empathy.

LOOK AT YOUR ACTIONS. Consider how your behavior may affect the relationship and find ways to improve.

LISTEN ACTIVELY. Pay full attention when someone speaks. Try to understand their point of view and respond thoughtfully.

SHOW APPRECIATION. Regularly express what you value about your partner.

BE OPEN TO FEEDBACK. Be ready to hear constructive criticism and use it to grow your relationships.

IT IS TIME TO LET GO OF A FRIENDSHIP, NO MATTER HOW LONG IT HAS BEEN. Friendships are essential in our lives. They provide support and companionship and boost our happiness and well-being. However, not all friendships last forever. As we move through different stages of life, our values, goals, and emotional needs can change a lot. This can lead to some friendships feeling out of sync. Holding on to a friendship just because of nostalgia or obligation can be harmful. It may cause stress, frustration, and emotional fatigue, lowering your quality of life. The energy you use to maintain a friendship that no longer benefits you can be better spent on healthier, more fulfilling relationships.

If you're unsure about a friendship, take time to think about its impact on your life. Here are eight signs that it may be time to end a friendship, regardless of how long you've known each other. Recognizing these signs can help you prioritize your emotional health and build better connections. Friendships matter. They shape who we are and influence our choices.

Chapter Nineteen

BIBLE VERSES ABOUT FRIENDSHIP THAT MAY HELP YOU CHOOSE GOOD FRIENDS AND KEEP YOUR FRIENDSHIPS STRONG

Proverbs 18:24 – "A man that hath friends must shew himself friendly: and there is a friend that sticketh closer than a brother."

This passage from Proverbs reminds us that friendships can be closer, more important relationships than family relationships. Friends can accompany us through moral and spiritual peril, just as Jesus Christ's disciples accompanied him.

Proverbs 17:17 – "A friend loveth at all times, and a brother is born for adversity."

This proverb conveys that genuine friendship is characterized by unconditional love.

While friendship may not demand unconditional approval of our actions, it should inspire us to see one another through the compassionate eyes of Jesus Christ.
John 15:13 – "Greater love hath no man than this, that a man lay down his life for his friends."

Jesus Christ imparted this profound lesson shortly before his death, exemplifying the ultimate expression of friendship. He loved with unwavering grace and boundless generosity.

Friendship inspires us to recognize the profound impact friends have on our thoughts, feelings, and actions. Just as one knife sharpens another, a true friend elevates us to become the best versions of ourselves. It's essential to choose friendship wisely, selecting those who will walk alongside us on our chosen path.

Ecclesiastes 4:9-10 – 'Two are better than one; because they have a good reward for their labor. For if they fall, the one will lift up his fellow: but woe to him that is alone when he falleth; for he hath not another to help him up."

This passage inspires us to recognize that we are not meant to be alone. As relational beings, we are gifted with one another for a purpose, to both offer support and embrace the help we receive.

Proverbs 27:9 – "Ointment and perfume rejoice the heart: so doth the sweetness of a man's friend by hearty counsel."

This proverb identifies one of the deepest sources of happiness we can find: Good, loving friendships that help us become better people.

1 Thessalonians 5:11 – "Wherefore comfort yourselves together, and edify one another, even as also ye do."

In this Bible verse, the apostle Paul beautifully illustrates the essence of true friendship. It embodies comfort and love, alongside edification. By embracing these qualities, friendship becomes a powerful teacher, revealing the will and character of God to all involved.

Job 16:20-21 – "My friends scorn me: but mine eye poureth out tears unto God. O that one might plead for a man with God, as a man pleadeth for his neighbor!"

The Book of Job tells of Job's despair and joy. For much of the book, Job is lectured by his friends for not obeying God well enough, though his friends have things wrong: it was not Job's actions that brought tragedy to him.

This passage from Job reminds us that friends may not always be right. We must remember that God is our ultimate exemplar and leader, not our friends.

Job 42:10 – "And the Lord turned the captivity of Job when he prayed for his friends: also, the Lord gave Job twice as much as he had before."

This verse also comes from Job in the Bible. Despite feeling harassed, Job prays on behalf of his friends. The Lord recognizes his generosity and strength and blesses him for it.

Proverbs 22:24-25 – "Make no friendship with an angry man; and with a furious man thou shalt not go: Lest thou learn his ways, and get a snare to thy soul."

These Bible verses about friendship counsel us to choose friends who will help us feel God's peace. People who cleave to darker emotions will often drag us down with them, further away from our relationship with God.

James 4:4 – "Ye adulterers and adulteresses, know ye not that the friendship of the world is enmity with God? whosoever, therefore, will be a friend of the world is the enemy of God."

In this Bible verse, the apostle James tells us to choose our friends wisely. Friendship with people who care more about the world than God or good values will likely lead us away from peace and joy.

Proverbs 16:28 – "A forward man soweth strife: and a whisperer separateth chief friends."

A "forward" man, as this Bible verse references, is an obstinate, stubborn man. Through His words and deeds, Jesus Christ sets an example of peacemaking, listening, and charity. We should find friends who also embody these virtues.

Colossians 3:13 – "Forbearing one another, and forgiving one another, if any man has a quarrel against any: even as Christ forgave you, so also do ye."

This passage from the book of Colossians reminds us that forgiveness and self-discipline are integral to loving relationships. No matter how hard we try, we will eventually hurt someone else, and someone else will eventually hurt us.

To preserve good relationships in the face of malice and thoughtlessness, we must try to refrain from annoyance and strive to forgive quickly and wholeheartedly.

Proverbs 27:6 – "Faithful are the wounds of a friend, but the kisses of an enemy are deceitful."

Like the teaching in Colossians 3:13, this Bible verse about friendship reminds us that friends who hurt us should not be judged as harshly as people who flatter us for deceitful ends.

Friends usually have good intentions, even if they hurt us or give us advice that strikes us as wrong. Enemies, however, will use any approach they can to pull us down. We should practice charity for our friends and try to listen to them while ignoring comments from those without good intentions.

1 Corinthians 15:33 – "Be not deceived: evil communications corrupt good manners."

This teaching from Paul to the people of Corinth identifies an element of friendship. Friendship includes kind speaking and generosity. A good friend will love you and build you up; to be a good friend, you must love someone and build them up.

Romans 12:10 – "Be kindly affectioned one to another with brotherly love; in honor preferring one another."

In this passage in the book of Romans, the apostle Paul essentially counsels us to act like we like our friends. He reminds us that friendship should help you feel good.

As in 1 Corinthians 15:33, this Bible verse about friendship reminds us that friendship should feel friendly. If someone never makes you feel good, they are not a true friend.

Philippians 2:3-4 - "Let nothing be done through strife or vainglory, but in lowliness of mind let each esteem other better than themselves. Look not every man on his own things, but every man also on the things of others."

These Bible verses about friendship remind us to invest sincerely in our friendships. Instead of entering into relationships with pride or condescension, we should love and cherish those around us.

Luke 6:31 – "And as ye would that men should do to you, do ye also to them likewise."

This Bible verse is the classic Golden Rule — do unto others as you would have them do unto you. Jesus Christ is teaching us that we should offer the same care and love that we would like to be treated with to others. This is the foundation of a good, mutually respectful friendship.

John 15:15 – "Henceforth I call you not servants; for the servant knoweth not what his lord doeth: but I have called you friends; for all things that I have heard of my father I have made known unto you."

In this scripture, Jesus Christ tells his disciples that they are his friends — and by extension, he calls us his friends, because he has also told us his mission and shared holy teachings.

1 Peter 4:8-10 – "And above all things have fervent charity among yourselves: for charity shall cover the multitude of sins. Use hospitality one to another without grudging. As every man hath received the gift, even so, minister the same one to another, as good stewards of the manifold grace of God."

In these Bible verses about friendship, the apostle Peter teaches that charity is the basis of friendship. It covers generosity, respect, and forgiveness. Furthermore, it is a gift from God.

When someone shows you charity, you feel the pure love of Jesus Christ. When you show someone else charity, you can draw from the pure love of Jesus Christ, too.

It's important to reassess and reframe your understanding of friendships and their significance in your life. Just because someone has been part of your upbringing since childhood does not inherently qualify them as a good friend; it simply means you have a lengthy shared history. This process of redefining your perceptions is a gradual but necessary step toward cultivating healthier, more stable, and genuinely authentic relationships.

Many of these long-standing friendships may carry emotional triggers that can elicit negative responses. Rather than reacting impulsively, seek out opportunities to respond calmly and constructively. Changing your mindset can significantly accelerate your healing journey from toxic relationships. Embrace the realization that you are now aware of how certain dynamics evoke feelings of distress or discomfort; this awareness is a crucial first step.

With this knowledge, it becomes your responsibility to actively manage and regulate your emotions and process what is truly happening with you in this relationship. It's imperative that you refrain from judging yourself for the impact that this friendship may have had on your emotional state. It is entirely valid to experience a range of emotions—whether it's anger, sadness, confusion, disorientation, or a sense of disorganization. See it and deal with it.

At this juncture, the practice of self-validation is far more powerful than self-judgment. Begin to acknowledge and affirm your feelings and experiences. Recognizing that it is perfectly normal to feel this way is not just beneficial; it is essential for your emotional well-being and personal growth. Allow yourself the grace to validate your feelings as you navigate this journey toward healthier relationships.

One of the (many!) unfortunate realities of adulting is that friendships can become challenging to hold on to as we age. Without school, club sports or college keeping you together, old friends can be hard to keep up with, especially as your lives travel down different paths at different paces. But experts believe we can still maintain these friendships, no matter what life throws at us, by practicing "gentle Sistah-hood."

You've most likely heard of gentle parenting, but the concept of "gentle Sistah-hood" — has only entered the chat relatively recently. To find out exactly what it means, and how we can use it to keep from losing those friendships that double as our lifelines, "'Gentle Sistah-hood' shares much of the same fundamentals as gentle parenting." "Rooted in understanding the other with empathy, validation, and problem-solving, 'gentle Sistah-hood' and gentle parenting may appear similar." The power dynamics of these two kinds of relationships really distinguish them, since friends don't depend on each other for survival the way a child depends on a parent.

While there is a key difference in power dynamics, we can apply the basic concepts of gentle parenting—including understanding, patience, and support—to our friendships and, hopefully, keep them strong and thriving.

The Key To 'Gentle Sistah-hoods'

Gentle Sistah-hoods, revolves around understanding and validating those closest to you, can help when it feels like maintaining a friendship is impossible in the face of life's chaos. The key to this process is keeping the important values of empathy, support, and problem-solving at the fore, even when your busy lives make it difficult.

The quality and quantity of social relationships can significantly impact health and well-being. Therefore, it is important to maintain friendships throughout different phases of life, even when both parties are busy. Although time may be limited, approaching these relationships with a supportive and abundant mindset is essential. It's important to make the other person feel emotionally seen and valued. Additionally, addressing problems without being influenced by external contexts or biases regarding what the other person may be experiencing is crucial for fostering long-lasting relationships.

When trying to be more empathetic towards your friends, it's important not to confuse empathy with simple people-pleasing. They are not the same. Empathy involves making a genuine effort to understand your friends' feelings and struggles in order to support them, rather than just saying or doing anything to keep them happy at your own expense. The goal is to help them feel seen and understood, with the hope that they will reciprocate that understanding for you as well.

Chapter Twenty

PUT 'GENTLE SISTAH-HOOD' INTO PRACTICE

Gentle Sistah-hood may seem like a simple concept, yet in reality, it presents a unique challenge for two best friends navigating the complexities of modern life. With the demands of work, the responsibilities of raising children, the intricacies of family dynamics, ongoing health concerns, financial struggles, and the ever-looming anxieties of our turbulent world, it becomes all too easy to lose sight of the importance of empathy and mutual support. Remembering to prioritize these elements can feel overwhelming, and translating that intention into action requires genuine effort.

In practice, 'Gentle Sistah-hood' often reveals itself not through grand, sweeping gestures, but through a myriad of small, meaningful acts of kindness. Whether it's sending a simple text to check in, sharing a moment of laughter over coffee, or providing a listening ear during tough times, these subtle yet impactful expressions of care foster a deeper bond. It's in these everyday moments that the essence of Sistahhood truly flourishes, illuminating the strength found in nurturing relationships amidst life's chaos.

"To cultivate and maintain vibrant friendships, even the smallest gestures can have a profound impact on the health of your relationships," "Taking a moment to send a text simply to ask how your friend is doing or sharing a funny meme that resonates with their sense of humor demonstrates that you genuinely care and are thinking of them."

The importance of remembering the little details in people's lives. Making a note of important events like birthdays, anniversaries, and milestones. Asking about specific stories or preferences during conversations can strengthen your relationships. He advises, "Asking about these details shows that you listen and supports your interest in their experiences."

We are all busy and taking time to reconnect is vital. Scheduling a FaceTime happy hour to enjoy a relaxing evening together or have a quick coffee catch-up at your favorite café. He believes these intentional gatherings, even if brief, can create a strong sense of connection that helps friendships last. "Spending this time together can really improve the quality of your relationship," he concludes.

Building and keeping healthy friendships as an adult takes effort, but it doesn't have to disrupt your busy life. Make it a habit to send a quick message or check in with your friends now and then. This simple act shows that you care. When you get messages, try to respond thoughtfully instead of leaving them unanswered.

Also, try to set aside time to hang out, even if it's not as often as you'd like. This could be a casual coffee once a month or a weekend outing every few months. Spending time together can strengthen your friendship and create lasting memories. If your friends are important to you, the effort you make to connect with them will enrich both your lives.

Chapter Twenty-One

AFFIRMATIONS

I am loving and accepting of others, creating lasting friendships for me.

I choose to have my life filled with positive people.

I have close friends who nurture me and make me laugh.

I make friends quickly with the positive people I attract.

I am open to friendship and have attracted the most beautiful new friends.

I am finding friends who are like-minded and appreciative of who I am.

My circle of friendships continues to grow beyond my expectations. I have an abundance of loving, supportive friends.

I have beautiful friends who are kind, loyal, supportive, and trustworthy.

I harmoniously resolve conflicts with my friends for the highest good within each of us.

Chapter Twenty-Two
REWARDS — CONCLUDING THOUGHTS -

Friendships, in all their forms, are essential for our well-being, and cultivating a diverse range of relationships can be highly beneficial. Friends play a crucial role in enhancing our mental health and supporting personal development. They also act as a protective barrier against negative experiences, such as emotional stress. While we recognize the significance of friendships, the exact mechanisms by which they impact our well-being are still not fully understood. Friendships activate specific areas of the brain associated with reward and motivation. Additionally, the process of friendship involves focusing on both oneself and others.

My Sistah friends mean everything to me. Friendships are crucial for fostering healthy and positive development in various aspects of life. They improve overall quality of life, alleviate symptoms of depression, reduce risky behaviors, and enhance academic performance. Furthermore, positive friendships can help diminish the effects of victimization and personal struggles. Ultimately, friends provide meaning to our lives, and often, the most unexpected friendships can be the most rewarding!

THE REWARDS

Rewards are positive experiences that encourage certain behaviors when people associate them with those actions. These rewards can be simple, such as enjoying your favorite food, or more complex, like spending time with a dear friend. This raises an important question: Are friendships special because they provide rewards? To explore this, a study examined brain activity during social interactions with friends.

BUILDING STRONGER

Relationships come in many forms, from family to friends and beyond. Even when you build strong connections with multiple people, the nature of each relationship will always differ. For example, you may not feel the same way about each parent, nor do you necessarily feel the same towards a loved one or partner as you do towards your friends. Each relationship is unique, and the feelings you have for different people vary as well.

Love is the foundational element of all relationships and friendships, yet the nature of that love can differ significantly from one connection to another. To cultivate a strong and enduring relationship, it is essential to wholeheartedly embrace the principles of love, authenticity, and honesty while actively being present for those you care about—particularly during their most challenging moments.

A crucial aspect of nurturing these connections is to maintain a nonjudgmental attitude toward one another. This allows individuals to express themselves freely without fear of criticism, fostering an environment of trust and understanding. It's important to recognize that it is impossible to make everyone happy; seeking universal approval can often lead to personal dissatisfaction. Instead, prioritize your own feelings and values to create authentic connections that resonate with your true self.

The ultimate aim should be to cultivate genuine Sistahhood, rooted in deep mutual respect and understanding. This involves not just surface-level interactions, but a commitment to truly listen and empathize with one another's experiences and perspectives. Focus on embodying kindness and compassion in your daily interactions—these qualities are fundamental in fostering and sustaining meaningful connections that bring joy and fulfillment to our lives.

It's important to recognize that not everyone we meet will become a close friend or partner. Therefore, it's essential to choose wisely when deciding which relationships to invest your time and energy in. Seek connections that are mutual and supportive, where both individuals feel valued and uplifted.

By thoughtfully selecting the connections you cultivate, you can create a strong Sistahhood that supports you and others. This intentional approach to building Sistah friendships can foster a Sistah community centered on empowerment, love, support, and most of all authentic Sisterhoods. Ultimately, this will nurture an environment where everyone feels valued, understood, and, most importantly, appreciated.

CONCLUDING THOUGHTS

Sistah Friendships are the most important ingredients in the receipt of life, and unexpected friendships are the best ones.

1. Every memorable moment out with Sistah friends will reduce the risk of loneliness and make life a little more enjoyable

2. With Sistah friends, you can talk about anything and everything. A listening ear provides solutions, support, and relief.

3. Sistah friends support our positive influence with others. They promote and share our contributions with others.

4. Shared laughter creates a bond. Instead of individuals, our Sistahs become a single group of human beings.

5. True Sistah friendships require sacrifices. These sacrifices make our lives much better.

6. Joy becomes more remarkable when we are Sistah friends and share together.

7. With Sistah friends, you can achieve anything! They can become the best partners in new endeavors.

- SISTAH FRIENDSHIP IS not keeping score.

- It's giving the benefit of the doubt.

- It's showing up for others and not waiting for them to appear first.

- It's giving the forgiveness you hope to get in return.

- It's cheering on and lifting up.

- It's listening and nodding.

- Good, secure Sistah friendship comes from a place of abundance, not scarcity.

- It's love, joy, and the abundance of life.

- Sistah friendship creates space for growth.

I believe that our connections with other women are essential for healing and personal growth. I have learned that friendships are not defined by the length of time we have known each other or the amount of time we spend together. Rather, they are about building deep relationships with people who inspire me to be better. These are the individuals who help me grow and make me feel safe, supported, and comfortable being myself.

You can meet a Sistah friend anytime, and real Sistah friendships happen in those moments. Some people will come to the party, while others will show up after it ends. Very few people will do both: truly get to know you and help you remember who you are when the world tries to take that away.

Sistah friendships can evoke a range of emotions, including support, loyalty, selflessness, fun, respect, kindness, companionship, heartbreak, miscommunication, laughter, and loss. At their core, these experiences are love stories. This is why I believe we should cherish friendships to the same status as romantic relationships. Our friends often provide the longest-lasting and closest connections in our lives, even though society tends to underestimate them.

Sistah friendship is where our most authentic selves can shine. These are the people with whom we can be completely ourselves, and they, for the most part, love us regardless. That attachment is more thrilling than any fairy tale.

I am thoroughly convinced that everyone "needs a Phoebe!" Having someone in your life like Phoebe is beneficial and rewarding. She brings a unique blend of positivity, quirkiness, and a lighthearted perspective, adding a fun and uplifting element to any situation; essentially, everyone could use a person who brings a bit of joyful chaos and unconventionality to their life.

Phoebe always sees the glass as half full, even during tough times, and her cheerful attitude is contagious. She has a creative spirit, coming up with unique ideas that lead to interesting conversations and effective problem-solving. Phoebe is genuine; she embraces her individuality and doesn't try to be like everyone else. Despite her sometimes-quirky behavior, she is compassionate and cares about others. You can always count on Phoebe, even in difficult situations.

I believe everyone should have a Phoebe in their lives because she has a great positive impact. Her unique perspective helps us see things we might miss, encouraging us to rethink our views. What makes Phoebe special is her ability to be herself without apology. She has a real talent for making people laugh, creating a fun atmosphere that feels personal and shared between just the two of you.

Phoebe's creativity is boundless. She often devises strange and imaginative concepts that spark our imaginations, turning the mundane into the extraordinary. Whether it's an outlandish theory about why the sky is blue or quirky suggestions for our weekend adventures, her ideas challenge us to think outside the box.

Phoebe is very protective and attentive. She makes sure I am well cared for and that my life feels balanced. Even with her own challenges, she stays optimistic and has a lighthearted attitude that brightens the mood of those around her. Her honesty is refreshing; she speaks her mind sincerely, showing genuine care for others.

Ultimately, having Phoebe in your life fosters an environment of love and authenticity, reminding us of the beauty of being true to ourselves and the importance of looking out for one another.

I thank the Lord for my Phoebes!!

Chapter Twenty-Three

PRAYER

Lord, You understand where I am in my life. I rely on Your grace and the power of the cross to release my hurt and to forgive those who have wronged me.

This moment marks a significant turning point in my life. I fully recognize my deep need for Your forgiveness, understanding that I have caused pain to others in the process. With a heartfelt sense of remorse, I sincerely apologize for my actions and their impact on those around me. I turn to You with confidence, choosing to extend forgiveness to those who have wronged me, just as You have so graciously forgiven my transgressions. As painful memories arise, I commit to the practice of forgiveness time and again, determined to transform that pain into a pathway toward healing and wholeness. I place my trust in Your boundless grace to mend my heart and soul. I realize that these lingering emotions have kept me imprisoned for too long, preventing me from experiencing true freedom. I humbly ask for Your divine strength to help me release the burdens of anger and hurt that weigh heavily upon me. Fill my heart, instead, with Your everlasting love and profound peace, guiding me toward a brighter future marked by compassion and understanding.

Holy Spirit, I humbly invite You to immerse Yourself in my life, working diligently to free me from the suffocating chains of bitterness that have held me captive for too long. Please begin a profound transformation within my heart, replacing resentment with compassion, and renewing my mind so that I may see the world through a lens of hope and understanding. Guide me towards true healing and reconciliation with myself and those I've struggled to forgive. I surrender every ounce of hurt and pain to You, placing my trust in the sufficiency of Your grace, which knows no bounds. May Your peace, which transcends all understanding, encircle my heart and guard my thoughts, leading me to the ultimate truth and knowledge in Christ Jesus. In His holy name, I pray for strength and guidance as I embark on this healing journey. Amen.

———

About the Author

Dr. LaWanna Harrod is the Founder and Director of the Christian Sistahs Foundation, also known as Sistahs in the City, and the CEO of Harrod Enterprises LLC. She earned her Doctorate from the Abundant Life Theological Seminary in Port St. Lucie, FL. LaWanna is a member of Shiloh Abundant Life Ministries in Forestville, where she serves as an Evangelist and Praise and Worship Leader.

As an author and publisher, she has written six books: "Junk in My Trunk," "The Fragmented Heart Healers," "21 Days with the Father," "I Won't Cry Past Tuesday," and "Lord, Move Me Into Betta." LaWanna is married to Robert Harrod, and they have two sons and six grandchildren.

Christian Sistahs Foundation, *hereinafter,*
Sistahs In The City
(240) 244-6502
www.SistahsintheCity.org
Sistahsinthecity@gmail.com

Sistahs In The City

If you're seeking a unique meetup experience to connect with new Sistah friends, Sistahs In The City would love to host a meet-and-greet, a Sistahs In The City Conference, or an online chat, please reach out @ sistahsinthecity@gmail.com or (240) 244-6502.